ON WINGS OF FAITH AND REASON

The John Henry Cardinal Newman Lectures

GENERAL EDITOR: *Craig Steven Titus*

The present collection of essays by recognized scholars in the fields of medicine, ethics, philosophy, and theology presents the work of the 2002–2003 John Henry Cardinal Newman Lecture Series. This Washington-based Lecture Series is held under the sponsorship of the Institute for the Psychological Sciences, and seeks to promote an international conversation among the several disciplines that treat the human person. The Newman Lecture Series is held annually, and forthcoming volumes will be published with an eye toward building a body of learned discussion that is catholic both in its breadth of research and in its dialog with contemporary Catholic thought. The published versions appear under the patronage of St. Catherine of Alexandria in order to demonstrate the conviction of those responsible for the Newman Lecture Series that the human person flourishes only when the Creator of heaven and earth is loved above all things.

The John Henry Cardinal Newman Lectures

VOLUME 2

ON WINGS OF FAITH
AND REASON

The Christian Difference in Culture and Science

EDITED BY *Craig Steven Titus*

The Institute for the Psychological Sciences Press
Arlington, Virginia

Distributed by
The Catholic University of America Press
620 Michigan Ave., N.E. / 240 Leahy Hall
Washington, DC 20064

The paper used in this publication meets the minimum requirements
of American National Standards for Information Science—Perma-
nence of Paper for Printed Library Materials, ANSI Z39.48-1984.
∞

LIBRARY OF CONGRESS CATALOGING-IN-PUBLICATION DATA
On wings of faith and reason : the Christian difference in culture and
science / edited by Craig Steven Titus.
        p. cm.—(John Henry Cardinal Newman lectures ; volume 2)
    Includes bibliographical references and index.
    ISBN-13: 978-0-9773103-3-3 (pbk. : alk. paper)   1. Christianity and
culture.   2. Religion and science.   I. Titus, Craig Steven, 1959–
    BR115.C80537 2008
    261.5—dc22   2007039135

CONTENTS

ACKNOWLEDGMENTS

In the name of the Institute for the Psychological Sciences, I would like to acknowledge the many actors who contributed to making this collection of essays possible. First of all, I would like to recognize the faithful generosity of Gene and Charlotte Zurlo, who have funded the John Henry Cardinal Newman Lecture Series from its inception. Furthermore, because of Dr. John Harvey's benevolent sponsorship, the lectures were held at the Cosmos Club (Washington, D.C.), which has continued to offer a fitting ambiance for genteel discussions. The corporate and personal authorities of the Institute for the Psychological Sciences (Arlington, Virginia) have warmly encouraged the publication of these lectures. Roman Lokhmotov and Cristina Melendez collaborated on creating the indices. Dr. David McGonagle (director), Elizabeth Benevides, and the rest of the staff of the Catholic University of America Press have contributed their competent and careful aid in bringing this volume to fruition. Finally, I would like to acknowledge the foresight of Prof. Daniel N. Robinson, who inspired this series, and the commitment and energy of Dean Gladys Sweeney, who mobilized a host of prominent scholars and organized the series and this publication.

Craig Steven Titus

ON WINGS OF FAITH AND REASON

Craig Steven Titus

INTRODUCTION

The revival of a perennial debate about the interplay of faith and reason has provoked some uncomfortable questions. If a scientific or cultural pursuit were to disdain reason or eschew faith, should the results be considered human advances or oddities? Are rational, scientific observations about the earth and trees, spiders and bees, great apes and human beings, necessarily at odds with the views of nature and humanity found in faith-based accounts? Lastly, could one responsibly choose to exclude, summarily, either reason or faith when discerning the commensurability of physical health, moral duty, and ultimate happiness?

With a shrug of the shoulder, many people would relegate faith and value-related issues to a private realm, while consigning facts born of reasoned observations to science; they thus avoid these questions. For confidence in the autonomy of science generally runs high, as does support for freedom and authenticity in expressions of values, culture, and personal taste. At the same time, philosophical and theological attempts to identify the presuppositions of science and of culture and to seek a coherent context for them have to bear the full burden of proof or be avoided. Nonetheless, while the practices of the natural or the human sciences might seem to be independent from

1

certain issues of ethics and faith, these sciences presume, willfully or not, a variety of linguistic uses, conceptual formulations, and foundational assumptions about the intelligibility of the world, as well as a worldview that requires the support of religious, agnostic, or atheistic faith. Even so, they often exempt themselves from the responsibility of identifying their own basic assumptions and agenda. Likewise, certain practices of culture assume immunity from standards of reason or faith; these infelicitous tendencies navigate toward a lowest common denominator or end in excess, even when they succeed in a striking achievement. Because of this general situation, foresight and honesty are needed in order to address the fundamental questions about the overarching context of the sciences and, especially, about the profound human desires to ponder beauty and to contemplate the ultimate meaning of life.

The difference that Christianity assures to questions about the interrelationship of culture and science, the writers in this volume purport, is that of a coherent vision of truth—a unifying truth that takes flight on the two wings of faith and reason. Against scientific reductionism, philosophical nihilism, and postmodern skepticism, such a vision affirms that the unity of truth is ultimate and personal and that the sciences and culture participate therein according to their own geniuses. This volume explores the service rendered by both faith and reason to the investigation of science and culture. It provides reasons for a unified vision of truth, while giving examples of the diverse tasks that faith and reason have in scientific activities and cultural expressions. In particular, its contributing authors—from the fields of medicine, ethics, philosophy, and theology—argue that Christianity makes a difference in culture and science, not only in providing an understanding of the ultimate origin and end of the human person, but in contributing to practical applications as well. Christianity proposes an assurance about the two-winged course of the investigation, while offering ample ground for creative expression and personal excellence in the investigation's execution.

Many have undertaken to pit faith against reason or reason against faith, but both undertakings are self-defeating. On the one hand, proponents of *sola fides,* such as Tertullian and Kierkegaard, set out to protect faith, without recognizing that any reflection upon faith avails itself, at least unwittingly, of rational concepts, linguistic constructs, and philosophical arguments. Reliable sciences, however, must nourish critical reason in the service of theological reflection, lest faith fall prey to an overly literal construal of Scripture or a historical-cultural naïveté. Against fideistic views, the contributions to this book argue that reason has a differentiated and positive part to play in theological investigations. As John Paul II averred in *Fides et Ratio,*[1] philosophical reflection should examine the intelligibility and truth-value of theological claims. The image of two wings, therefore, does not intimate that faith and reason exercise the same role in a unified flight of knowledge; nor does it mean that faith can substitute itself for reason; nor should it suggest that isolated one-dimensional theories of truth will satisfy.

On the other hand, proponents of *sola ratio,* such as Descartes and Kant, set out to protect reason, without recognizing that reason's autonomy need not deny the autonomy proper to revealed faith. To say "reason" is not to restrict oneself to philosophy construed as a quite limited branch of knowledge. Rather, the sciences, as the fruit of logical and measured observation, a rigorous principled inquiry, are also the work of reason. Philosophy and the sciences work within the order of natural reason.[2] For the ancients, the study of natural sciences in large part coincided with philosophical inquiry.[3] At present, however, the technical precision of the various methods refined for each

1. Pope John Paul II, *Fides et Ratio* (*FR*—Encyclical on *Faith and Reason,* September 14, 1998), n. 77; see also n. 65ff.

2. As John Paul II explains in *Fides et Ratio* (n. 9), "Philosophy and the sciences function within the order of natural reason; while faith, enlightened and guided by the Spirit, recognizes in the message of salvation the 'fullness of grace and truth' (cf. Jn 1:14) which God has willed to reveal in history and definitively through his Son, Jesus Christ (cf. 1 Jn 5:9; Jn 5:31–32)."

3. *Fides et Ratio,* n. 19: "For the ancients, the study of the natural sciences coincided in large part with philosophical learning."

natural and human science is daunting. Who can pronounce on any one of the sciences without extensive training? Moreover, the compartmentalization of knowledge has led to skepticism about the complementariness of all quests for truth and especially the inclusion of philosophy and theology therein. Against rationalist views, this volume argues not only that faith builds up reason without making it a-rational or irrational, but also that it is a source of knowledge, the denial of which restricts not only our passive reception and active observation of reality, but also our creative responses to it.

In the name of controlled method, the modern sciences have focused on material causes; for its part, culture has focused on subjective personal experience. Both have often restricted the boundaries of what they consider rational, thereby concealing an objective basis for creative action (that is, freedom), a teleological purpose in human life, and a divine source of truth. First, physical and natural sciences acknowledge certainty only in terms of mathematical and empirically verifiable methods. They rightly limit and direct their studies, which focus on analysis of the orderliness inherent in nature. In particle physics, for example, such focus and application have produced spectacular discoveries concerning the elements that constitute our world (without yet producing a "theory of everything" in physics). When, however, they claim to possess the only valid method for arriving at trustworthy knowledge, proponents of science overstate their own competency or that of their method. For example, E. O. Wilson argues for a "hierarchical ordering of knowledge that unites and drives the natural sciences,"[4] but he denies that this ordering could include philosophy, theology, or the human sciences (with perhaps the excep-

---

4. E. O. Wilson, *Consilience: The Unity of Knowledge* (New York: Vintage Books, 1998), 198. Wilson's theory of "consilience," or the unity of knowledge, favors a bottom-up synthesis based on biological and psychological empiricism (the former grounded in physics and chemistry). Wilson admits that this rational inquiry might satisfy the mind, but will be thwarted by the movement of the heart, which seeks the transcendental solutions offered in revelation and religion.

tion of experimental psychology). He excludes not only faith and any reasons for faith, but also rational arguments that are not based on experimental and mathematical methods. Now, without denying the immense value of science, we may confidently state that such a claim to absolute autonomy is vain.

For their part, the human sciences seek material descriptions or functional explanations of the subjective and the social. Practitioners of these sciences can overstep boundaries in two directions: (1) they can fail to recognize that their studies rest upon and use fundamental presuppositions and guiding principles, and (2) their speculation can outstrip their competency. The first constitutes a type of false independence, the second a type of free license.

In a nonreductionist view of the sciences, by contrast, a relative but complete autonomy fits each science to its inherent dignity, methodological boundaries, and proper goals. Philosophy's autonomy is rooted in the fact that reason is naturally oriented to truth and is equipped to arrive at it.[5] Philosophy does not achieve or protect its autonomy by hermetically sealing itself off from the findings of other sciences and from the premises of faith. In his lecture "Christianity and Medical Science" (1858), John Henry Cardinal Newman provides insights into the ordering of the sciences that concern the human person. Employing a nonmaterialist and nondualist body-soul anthropology, he appreciates the relative sovereignty of the mind and soul in the whole person. He can thus say that

> bodily health is not the only end of man, and the medical science is not the highest science of which he is the subject. Man has a moral and religious nature, as well as a physical one. He has a mind and a soul; and the mind and the soul have a legitimate sovereignty over the body, and the sciences relating to them have in consequence the precedence of those sciences which relate to the body.[6]

5. *Fides et Ratio,* n. 49.

6. John Henry Cardinal Newman, *The Idea of a University* (1858; New York: Image Books, 1959), 456.

While each science expresses valid truths, a synthetic science super-sedes rather than confutes the truth of the more analytical science. As Newman says: "Who will deny that health must give way to duty?"[7] What is true or fact, as knowable or achievable in one science, may not be lawful in practice, because of considerations and determina-tions of a higher normative science—in particular, political, moral, and religious ones. Conscience will rightfully follow the higher road.

In the name of truth (or at least validity), academic methodologi-cal canons do impose their own rigor, but they need not beg the ques-tion against theological considerations or reduce the field of inquiry to insignificant ruminations about parts of parts of parts, never re-turning to the whole living being at hand or to the synthetic question of the whole of reality. The rigor of a discipline is properly construed as a limited autonomy that does not efface either the competencies of other disciplines (or branches of knowledge) or the need for a larger synthetic vision.[8]

In the name of reason and at the expense of faith, western culture has witnessed a certain de-hellenization of science, which has been mathematically, historically, and culturally redefined. As reported by Pope Benedict XVI in his Regensburg lecture,[9] three successive stages have recast science in models that dissect and limit the full unity of knowledge. The result is various islands of knowledge separated by mathematical, historical, and cultural methodologies that are indif-ferent to each other. Lamenting the distance between the sciences is one thing, building a bridge another. Benedict XVI promotes a rap-

7. Ibid.

8. Therefore, it need not exclude some sort of humble opening toward contribu-tions from other disciplines, especially when studying the human person and the reli-gious or the transcendental potential. An optimistic read will affirm that many scien-tists have not lost humility and perspective. Nonetheless, certain prominent thinkers, considered sage in our times, miss this more inclusive mark by a reductionist and ob-fuscating tendency. For example, Richard Dawkins, *The God Delusion* (New York: Houghton Mifflin, 2006); Steven Rose, *Lifelines: Biology, Freedom, Determinism* (Ox-ford: Oxford University Press, 1997); or E. O. Wilson, as already mentioned.

9. Pope Benedict XVI, Lecture at the University of Regensburg (September 12, 2006).

prochement between biblical faith and Greek-style philosophical inquiry, while recognizing that this revival demands the integration of modern scientific advances into a larger vision.

How, then, are the canons of reason and faith related to the natural sciences, the human sciences, philosophy, and theology? How is it that all scientific and cultural efforts are ordered, together, in a quest toward truth? Aquinas would have us distinguish a twofold order of knowledge within this unified quest,[10] but without creating any dualism of person or science. A single thirst for truth is manifest in the multiplicity of disciplines. On the one hand, all the sciences except theology have in common the recourse to reasoned observation, theory-driven inquiry, self-corrective use of hypotheses, and so on. These sciences employ reason in manifold quantitative and qualitative methods in order to focus on various aspects of reality. Classically speaking, the sciences and philosophy have been seen as different ways of focusing human natural reason in observation and reflection on different objects of study. On the other hand, the experimental, practical, and speculative sciences (which is to say, the natural and human sciences, including philosophy) differ from properly theological sciences by virtue of their sources, objects, and methods of examination. Theological investigation employs revelation as the primary, proper, but not exclusive source for its consideration of the truths about God and about creation in relation to God.[11] It starts by a receptive listening to faith *(auditus fidei)* and then develops through a

10. See Romanus Cessario, "Twofold Order of Knowledge: *Duplex Ordo Cognitionis,"* in P. J. Griffiths and R. Hütter, eds., *Reason and the Reasons for Faith* (New York: T and T Clark, 2005), 327–38.

11. Aquinas discusses the use of Scripture, patristic texts, and philosophical-scientific works as authorities in theological reflection in his treatment of whether sacred doctrine is a matter of argument; see *Summa theologiae* Ia, q. 1, a. 8, ad 2. He explains that, first, theology draws its "proper and necessary" arguments *(proprie, ex necessitate argumentando)* from the authority of canonical Scripture; second, its "proper, but probable" arguments *(quasi arguendo ex propriis, sed probabiliter)* are derived from the authority of doctors of the Church; and third, its "extrinsic and probable" arguments *(quasi extraneis argumentis, et probabilibus)* come from the authority of philosophers (among whom we would include scientists in various levels).

speculative inquiry of faith *(intellectus fidei)* that demands the use of reason in seeking the warrants of faith.[12] In this view, the research results that emanate from either *fides* or *ratio* neither duplicate nor exclude the other, but rather are complementary; "the truth attained by philosophy and the truths of revelation are *neither identical nor mutually exclusive,*" as John Paul II says.[13]

Distinguishing the sciences by source, object, and method, however, tells us only one chapter in this story. There is a popular thirst not only for detailed parts of the picture of life, but also for a macro vision, a unity of knowledge. In particular, there is interest in bypassing tendentious distinctions between the subjective and the objective study of the human person in order to perceive the person and society in function of our biopsychosocial and spiritual unity of being.

We can address, moreover, at least one of the other key questions of method and ordering of the sciences by addressing the issue of service. The question "How do the sciences and branches of knowledge serve each other?" has become taboo, since the modern notion of science has rendered absolute the notion of its autonomy and at the same time has restricted the notions of unity or correlation and of mutual service. However, without deprecating the diversity of the sciences, more and more scientists admit that no science is an island. Each science takes as its presuppositions the findings of another. Such presuppositions are construed as nonverifiable from within the receiving discipline. Nonetheless, these (relative) starting points lead to the speculation and application that is specific to the host discipline.

---

12. *Fides et Ratio* (n. 65) explains these two moments: "Theology is structured as an understanding of faith in the light of a twofold methodological principle: the *auditus fidei* and the *intellectus fidei*. With the first, theology makes its own the content of Revelation as this has been gradually expounded in Sacred Tradition, Sacred Scripture and the Church's living Magisterium (cf. Second Vatican Ecumenical Council, Dogmatic Constitution on Divine Revelation *Dei Verbum,* n. 10). With the second, theology seeks to respond through speculative inquiry to the specific demands of disciplined thought."

13. *Fides et Ratio,* n. 9.

The idea of service does not destroy the principle of the relative autonomy of the sciences. At different periods in the history of science (in the large sense of the word, as a rigorous principled inquiry), different views on the links between these disciplines have held sway.[14] Aristotle held that the experimental sciences served first philosophy *(prima philosophia)* or metaphysics. St. Justin Martyr was one of the Church Fathers who recognized the place of non-Christian (or pagan) philosophy in the expression and defense of the truths of religion. St. Albert the Great and St. Thomas Aquinas steeped themselves in the wisdom of classical pagan sources, at all the levels of philosophy and science; in particular, they recognized the valid autonomy of these sciences, which made indispensable contributions to theology. The notion of service found in these thinkers—as distinct from the practice of the sciences in compartmentalized academic fiefs—does not deny the value of a discipline that needs the findings of another, nor does it deny the value of a discipline that renders its work to another; that is, being at the service of another discipline and being served by another discipline are qualities of science.

Let us now turn to the services rendered by the contributing authors in their refined conversation about faith, reason, and the Christian different in science and culture.

Edmund Pellegrino, from his experience as a medical doctor and bioethicist, presents the challenges of Catholic education in the applied domains of medicine and bioethics. He employs Cardinal Newman's *Idea of a University,* in which he reflects on his experience as

---

14. "It was because of its noble and indispensable contribution that, from the Patristic period onwards, philosophy was called the *ancilla theologiae.* The title was not intended to indicate philosophy's servile submission or purely functional role with regard to theology. Rather, it was used in the sense in which Aristotle had spoken of the experimental sciences as 'ancillary' to *'prima philosophia.'* The term can scarcely be used today, given the principle of autonomy to which we have referred, but it has served throughout history to indicate the necessity of the link between the two sciences and the impossibility of their separation." *Fides et Ratio,* n. 77.

rector at the Catholic University of Ireland in Dublin (1854–1858) as the historical backdrop and intellectual overview for the essay. Pellegrino explains the pertinence of Newman's views on the dangers and possibilities that face the effort of Catholic liberal arts and medical education. Newman has a very acute sense of the antagonism that pits liberal and professional (practical) educations against each other. The decisive issue is their compatibility and ordering.

First of all, Newman warned against the arrogance and reduction that are often endemic to the natural sciences (especially the life sciences) and the practical sciences (especially medicine). He also worried that their clarity and achievements could blind people to the dignity of the human person. His times were shaped by the strong winds of scientific positivism. The advances in physics and biology seemed to promise sciences that were sure and that were necessarily autonomous, in order to carry out their investigation free of interference. Newman rightly cautioned his audience that erroneous presuppositions in medicine construe physical health as the highest human good, confuse scientific truths with what is morally licit in practical research and medical practice, and confound scientific findings (and theories) with the final explanation of reality.

However, Newman warmed to the potential of a medical faculty in a Catholic university. He even came to believe that it had a critical role there. In contrast to the numerous potential pitfalls, he developed principles that aid ongoing reflection on the possibility of Catholic medical education (and other practical disciplines such as psychotherapy and applied arts) in a pluralistic context. In order to overcome the shortcomings of applied sciences, Newman foresaw the need for physicians and scientists to be learned both in their faith and in science. The goals for Newman's university and what he called a liberal education were twofold. *First*, education is based in human reason and pursues the intellectual flourishing of the human person. The primary end of university education is that the person acquire intellectual discipline for its own sake; professional and scientific educations

are secondary. The liberal arts thus serve as a foundation and propaedeutic for the study of theology, medicine, law, and the sciences, and
for every good path of life. *Second,* he promoted a dialogue between
science and religion and culture. He hoped that theological reflection
would inform the Catholic physician's approach to the medical science and that the medical doctors in turn would inform theological
reflection with references to scientific advances. One of the roles of
the Catholic university was cultural evangelization. Concerning the
medical school, Newman thought that it would provide the means to
engage certain of the philosophical, ethical, and religious challenges
posed by the sciences.

Between 1854 and 1858, in no small way due to his contact with
the school of medicine, Newman's thought matured, as is seen in
three lectures that he gave as rector: "Christianity and Physical Science" (1854), "Christianity and Scientific Investigation," and "Christianity and Medical Science" (1858). His basic insights spring from his
conception of the unity of truth, which requires patient investigation
and an ordered relationship of the disciplines in order to reconcile the
sciences. As Newman said, medicine is found at the crossroads between advances in biology and life sciences, on the one hand, and traditional morals and beliefs, on the other. It can serve as a bridge between science and religion.

Pellegrino affirms that the impact of medical practice will be determined by the quality of its vision of human dignity, as based in being
created in the image of God. Education to this vision involves not only
a philosophical and theological anthropology, but also its application
in medical ethics. Dr. Pellegrino applies Newman's prescient vision and
remarks to the contemporary situation, calling on the insights of John
Paul II's reflections on education, culture, and ethics. In the doing, he
identifies six elements for this medical education in Catholic universities: (1) moral courage to resist conformist pressures of the modern
academy, especially concerning human life issues; (2) intellectual education as a propaedeutic for all other studies; (3) exposure to rigor-

ous philosophical and theological training in order to master ethics in practice; (4) comprehensive education in the life sciences, according to one's specialization; (5) a critical sense based in natural law and human dignity in order to decipher different points of view; and (6) a capacity to make judgments in both secular and Christian bioethics. The mastery of scientific, religious, and ethical speculative knowledge and practical judgments is a high order, to be purchased not by simple discourse but by hard-earned education. But such excellence and engagement with modern culture is the only fitting goal for the human person and society.

The use of and the relation between reason and faith are at the heart of many burning debates today, such as that pitting intelligent design theorists against neo-Darwinian accounts of humankind. Such debates at different levels involve efforts that are properly differentiated as observation, speculation, and revelation. In Kevin L. Flannery's contribution, he asks whether the renowned two wings of theology and philosophy that John Paul II identifies in *Fides et Ratio* can be personified by the thought of Aristotle and Aquinas respectively in order to illustrate how the philosopher's knowledge and the theologian's knowledge about the temporal creation of the world and about grace serve as test cases about the relationship of these two disciplines. Can we know with certainty and through logical arguments and empirical observations that the world either was created in time or has existed eternally? Flannery practices Aquinas's arguments to show that faith need not and indeed cannot stand alone in these matters. An author's right conclusion, which might have been furnished by faith, need not mean that he has rightly argued against opposing positions, nor for correct practical applications. Flannery aids us in understanding the proper use of propositional argumentation in speculative affairs that press the boundaries of experience and reason, such as in regard to the creation of the world. The normal course of causal inquiry seeks the cause(s) of an effect, that is, of concrete events; but the search for the intermediate causes of a proximate cause and for the first cause of the whole series demands attention to whether trusted methods of analysis hold as usual. In the case of creation, according to Aquinas and Moses Maimonides, we need to resist the inclination to imagine that the event is like other more common ones. It is not like events that we understand because we can grasp when they begin and finish. For can we clearly respond to the question: when did the *beginning* finish? On the one hand, Aristotle's philosophical argument for the eternity of the world is based on his concept of time, which is defined as the end of the past and the beginning of the future. The philosopher reasons that each present moment is preceded by a past moment, which was a present moment at one time. This temporal chain regresses eternally as does the world itself. Aristotle here, according to Aquinas and Maimonides, has transgressed logic. In this case, Flannery explains, Aristotle's definition begs the question. Thus Aquinas makes recourse to higher reasons or principles in order to clarify the relationship of the definition (or principle) to reality. In this cosmological realm, arguments based on definitions alone are not conclusive. Instead of being proofs, they are beliefs. For philosophical, logical argumentation aids us to organize things that we already know by other means. Theology, on the other hand, as Joseph de Finance affirms, gives us more information. Although there is no human witness to creation in time, through sacred Scripture properly interpreted God does reveal that the world has a temporal origin. This discussion does not stop Aquinas from affirming that Aristotle has another doctrine about creation that holds true. While creation in time demands revelation, the knowledge that the world depends upon God for its very being depends upon good definitions and proper understanding of the metaphysical structure of their referents. Thus the causal structure of the world indicates that forms are more intelligible than matter. There is more intelligibility in higher forms, such as a dog, than in the lower forms that compose it, such as the forms of flesh and bones, calcium and sodium, and so on. However, this intelligibility implies a higher one, since we can bring under control parts or expressions of human nature (such as thoughts and emotions), but we cannot give intelligibility to our nature itself. Rather a higher, more intelligible source, which must be an intellect, must be its creator. Flannery does not treat the arguments of neo-Darwinians or creationists, but in an irenic fashion he does set out the principles of causality and intelligibility that could be used to clear many misunderstandings.

Another pressing issue concerns supernatural grace and people who do good things without the virtue of practical wisdom. Aristotle, in the *Eudemian Ethics* (book VII, chapter 8), argues that some other impulses, besides natural human capacities of practical wisdom, order the person to good things. He holds that the causal ordering of the universe leads the ardent thinker right back to God, who is the ultimate cause of the universe and of motion in the human soul. This source of reason is something greater than reason. Aquinas (*Summa theologiae* Ia-IIae q. 68, a. 1) employs Aristotle's thought here in order to explain divine inspiration and the gift of the Holy Spirit. He presses the Philosopher's thought into service in order to explain that there are two sources for human action—human and divine reason. What does this tell us about the "two wings on which the human spirit rises to the contemplation of truth"? Philosophers, such as Aristotle, can come to know that grace exists and that God as creator is the source of intelligibility. Nonetheless, they lack information to which theologians are privy, as believers. In particular, they lack the full import of divine grace; especially that even the grace apparent in the unbeliever is mediated through Jesus Christ, sacred Scripture, and his Church. This information is divine information, not philosophy. Flannery thus makes a case that the Church's mission requires both theology and philosophy and demands that each discipline not exclude the other in order to present faith reasonably and in a balanced way. He accentuates the distinction between faith and reason, an effort that allows us nonetheless to recognize further their interaction and the unity of human search for truth.

Jude Dougherty displays a confidence in the possibility of reason to attain truth, but also to display error. He masterfully traces the contours of the different ways that philosophers and theologians have related reason to faith and faith to reason. The tableau is nuanced. The extremes strike the eye, even as the harmonious middle ground soothes the mind and invites contemplation of the constructive relationship between faith and reason, as structured within a realist conception of creation and salvation, nature and grace, even ecumenical friendship.

However, some would have it that the risk of error discredits philosophy from having a place in theology, or alongside it. Tertullian, for example, penned diatribes against Aristotle, whom he considered both wretched and obsolete. With the Gospels in hand, why endanger Christian apologetics and biblical exegesis with classical learning or with Greco-Roman philosophy? This view did not simply pass away after Tertullian in the second and third centuries. It has resurfaced in various thinkers who have expressed anti-metaphysical and fideistic views, such as Luther, Kierkegaard, and the latter's more recent disciples Barth, Bultmann, and Tillich. Certain philosophers for their part, such as the British empiricists, have further undermined confidence in reason's capacity to know something of the unseen from the seen; others, such as Kant and Enlightenment philosophers in general, have sought to undercut any rational preamble for faith. Explorations about the nature of religious belief came to base themselves on the human subject as opposed to the world. In resistance to Hegel's rationalism, Kierkegaard made a unique place for himself in modern times; he consolidated the turn to the inwardness of the subject with a turn away from scientific accounts of the world. Faith needs neither science nor philosophy; rather it must affirm both objective uncertainty and subjective truth.

Dougherty's historical sketch gives way to considerations of contemporary trends in which philosophers offer strong words of challenge to theology. In many circles—including Catholic colleges and seminaries—the result is to undercut attempts at coherent rational discourse of a systematic bent (universally applicable discourse). Any pretension of rational coherence (of larger patterns of coherence) is eschewed, or belittled as misguided and archaic. Analytical critiques sever experiential muscle from philosophical bone, and this rational bone from theological marrow, leaving the human victim dissected, without hope of finding unity in belief, reason, or experience. This sacrifice serves no good or human purpose except to undo pretentious efforts (including the Enlightenment model), with a Wittgensteinian critique that offers a first step toward reappropriating premodern and postmodern efforts at recognizing the unity of truth.

What can be culled from these lessons is that when considering the stance of faith, one needs a critique that demonstrates the limits of each school of philosophy. A measured use of philosophy has been promoted by numerous eminent philosopher-theologians of the Church: philosophy can provide intellectual tools to understand and defend the faith (Justin Martyr); Christian philosophy can expose and eliminate what is false in rational discourse, as well as guide people to Christ and elucidate his teachings (Clement of Alexandria). Here there is no confusion of the role of philosophy and theology, but a confidence that reason can aid theological reflection and that faith is not unreasonable. John Paul II's encyclical *Fides et Ratio* (1998) is a part of this trend, as is displayed by his opening words: "Faith and reason are like two wings on which the human spirit rises to the contemplation of truth." Without claiming that the Church has one official philosophy, John Paul II, like Leo XIII in *Aeternae Patris* (1879) before him, proposes St. Thomas Aquinas's synthetic treatment of reason and faith as a model for imitation. As Dougherty points out, this effort seeks not only to master the tradition but also to engage the secular and other Christian mindsets.

This remedy involves realist educative efforts and an ordering of the sciences that is open to the unifying role of truth in faith and reason. Dougherty takes the need for establishing foundations for ethics as a case in point. If the realist ethicist argues in a restricted sense, using only the lowest common denominator, he leaves his arguments exposed to the dead ends of modernity. Accepting uncritically secular terms and only certain supposedly noncontroversial starting points—such as John Rawls's proposed inalienable value to human life—makes for an exercise in frustration. Without deeper foundations and other pertinent principles, it is difficult to demonstrate the limitations of a harmonious but errant system (such as that of Rawls). In the current culture that has lost many of its Christian references, the Church is in a situation that is not unlike that of the first centuries of the Christian era. An ever more secular society needs to be recognized as such. And the tools of faith and reason need to be employed not only to critique errors, but to explore the truths that reason and faith can lay before us as so many ways to recover and advance the Christian intellectual heritage.

What difference does Christian faith make in understanding personal relationships? Robert Sokolowski demonstrates that this is not simply a logical question, nor one that remains at the level of the individual. Employing the insights of eminent German Catholic philosopher Robert Spaemann, he first explores the conception and uses of the word "person" in order to understand this difference. "Person" exhibits a distinct usage from the term "human being." In the dictum of philosophers of language, "human being" is a "sortal" term, which sorts out a certain species, *homo sapiens,* from other genera of living things. Moreover, terms such as "human being" are universals, which can have a multitude of individuals as members of the species that exist, live, walk, and talk, in the case of the human individual. "Person," on the other hand, is not a sortal term. Like the demonstrative pronoun "this," "person" is radically individualized every time we use the word. Its logic implies singularity, as well as a rational status and dignity that makes "person" in a certain way incommunicable. Furthermore, "person" helps to explain how the human being is more radically individualized than are other animals, which do not have the same potential to shape their own character. However, Sokolowski recognizes that there is a challenge in reconciling the two terms, for distinguishing "human being" (or man) from "person" can lead to two extreme interpretations. First, a reductionist perspective might construe them in a dualist light, as if the two terms expressed two separate things in us, one opposed to the other. Second, an existentialist extreme would detach the human being (as human nature) from the person, who is capable not only of governing himself, but also of radically creating himself as he sees fit. As a middle way, Sokolowski works out a distinction that avoids separating human being from person, and both of them from human nature by which we must govern ourselves. In particular, he affirms that human rational capacities make us persons and that reason singularizes the human being, making us not only members of a species but distinct subjects. In this perspective, spirit—manifest by human rational powers—adds further sense to the word "soul," which as a principle of vital unity is common to every living thing. With phenomenological flair, Sokolowski describes how human reason is exhibited by cognition and by action as well. In the domain of cognition, judgments express not only that human beings possess cognitive reason, but that they are persons. In particular, the declarative use of the first person singular (such as "I think that he is telling the truth") phenomenologically reveals the human person. In the domain of action, we manifest our rationality and personhood in the way that we become responsible and can be praised and blamed for our acts. What is distinctive of the human person is the capacity to govern oneself and proactively cultivate a life according to nature. It is thus that Spaemann says that a human being "has a nature. Nature does not have him."[15] Nonetheless, human persons do not learn alone how to make judgments, nor do we teach ourselves how to act. Other persons are needed in each person's actu-

15. Robert Spaemann, *Personen: Versüche über den Unterschied zwischen "etwas" und "jemand"* (Stuttgart: Klett-Cotta, 1996), 105, as quoted by R. Sokolowski here following.

alization of his or her cognitive and moral potential. The human capacity to judge is born of the observations, opinions, and judgments that other cognitive agents have made in our presence. The baby and child experience many judgments before attaining the sophistication to do the same; this takes place in the family, with friends, and in larger circles of social interaction. A person's mind is activated to be an agent of truth only in reciprocity with other people. This intersubjectivity, which makes human judgments possible, is another expression of personhood. Moreover, human moral action develops virtuously only through the social interaction found in the guidance of others and in a central way in friendship. Friendship, for Aristotle as well as for Sokolowski, is the accomplishment of human nature; it implies the plenitude of the virtues, as so many forms of friendship with self (courage and temperance) and others (justice).

On this philosophical foundation, Sokolowski discusses how Christian faith modifies personal relationships. Sokolowski sketches how the doctrines of the creation, Incarnation, and Holy Trinity influence our understanding of the human person and our relationships. While Aristotle saw a natural rift between man and god with no friendship possible, Christian faith, as expressed in the Gospel of St. John, introduces the truth about the relationship between Christ and the Father, and thus offers a new kind of friendship. The originality of this offer of friendship does not, however, draw attention away from God. Rather it opens new possibilities of obedience and even affirmations about our relationship with God. Moral and religious conduct is shaped by the Christian understanding of friendship. For example, using the first-person singular pronoun, we can say "I believe" and "I love," and thus enter into an order of exchange not possible by natural endowments alone. We are enabled to act as agents of truth, reflecting the native generosity and charity alive in the Godhead. Through such a high vocation of imitating the self-giving of Christ and the interpersonal love of the Trinity, the natural virtues are not overridden but seen to have an internal logic that can be made to participate in the goodness of God.

This message confirms human relationality and reason while raising us to new kinds of relationship, knowledge, and belief.

Neither despair nor discouragement is warranted in the midst of the current cultural winter and rough going for families. Although "the world grows old, the Church is ever young." Richard John Neuhaus takes inspiration from these words of Cardinal Newman to recognize and encourage a second springtime in the Church at present. In particular, Neuhaus emphasizes the prophetic humanism of John Paul II's timely message for spiritual renewal. Instead of despair and discouragement, hope, courage, and even joy are called for, in the springtime of the Church that sets itself to the work of evangelizing and re-evangelizing, supporting and even transforming its members, families, and culture. In the midst of no small amount of confusion and counterindications, the fallow time will give way to new growth through five pressing transformations to be realized in the life of the Church. Cultivating intelligently the courage to stand for truth and act for right even against generalized cultural trends will make for Catholics who can offer authentic contributions to advance contemporary culture. The remedy to cultural ailments involved in the call to moral greatness and holy lives recurs in John Paul II's message to young and old alike: "Settle for nothing less than moral and spiritual greatness." Without imposing itself, the Church proposes the way of fidelity to Christ that passes by fuller appropriation of the gift of Peter (the papacy) and Catholic truth and unity. This message goes hand in hand with the Church's coherent teaching on sexuality, marriage, and family, which involves understanding how conjugal love and the conjugal act relate to the whole invitation to holiness and to honor marriage as a Christian vocation. Lastly, Neuhaus indicates that we need an intense commitment to a politics of family as outlined in the Church's *Charter of Family Rights* (1983) and in John Paul II's encyclical *Familiaris Consortio (FC)*.[16] Indeed the prophetic humanism of

16. *The Role of the Christian Family in the Modern World* (Apostolic Exhortation, November 22, 1981).

John Paul II has proposed that "humanity's passage to the future is through the family" (*FC,* n. 86); Neuhaus encourages us to take family seriously without shortchanging its moral and spiritual levels.

The perennial philosophical-moral question concerns happiness. Doesn't everyone seek it, in one form or another? Even in the worst-case scenario because of physical illness, psychological pathology, or social oppression, when the most commonly held aspects of flourishing are impossible, don't we at least try to decrease unhappiness? Great thinkers have anguished over happiness, building whole syntheses of thought upon it (Aristotle and Aquinas), trying to measure and maximize it (Bentham, Mill, and the other utilitarians), or, especially when happiness is identified with power or pleasure (hedonism), attempting to discredit it as a danger to public morality (Kant and deontological ethicists). Different people have confused true happiness (or blessedness) with contentment for lack of clear distinction concerning the good and the apparent, responsibility and fortune, the long and the short term, objective fact and subjective feeling. Peter Kreeft treats happiness in the context of the post-Christian West and its contrast with Christ's concept of happiness. The Christian position does not exaggerate the moat that separates the ancient, modern, and postmodern conceptions, since it recognizes the possibility that objective perfection can coincide with subjective satisfaction, although it might not exclude personal suffering. A contemporary view that predominates in Western culture would put nine ingredients into its formula for happiness: wealth, lack of suffering, technological advancement, self-esteem, justice and rights, sexual and ecstatic pleasure, success, acceptance, and health. Don't these impregnable values receive universal acclaim? In this context, Kreeft takes us on a thought experiment: try to imagine how the opposite of these nine values might become the backbone of the most popular book of the most famous teacher. Difficult! Any questioning of these apparently encrusted values seems inhuman. Doesn't the constant and natural appeal of these values make them patent proofs against any opponent? Upon closer inspection, as Kreeft cues us, these values, when taken as absolutes in themselves, defy point by point the Beatitudes of Jesus' Sermon on the Mount. The rub, of course, is in the conception of true happiness. Rather than shying away from the Sermon on the Mount as irretrievable baggage from the distant past, as hyperbolic rhetoric, or as poetic abstraction, Kreeft takes the Beatitudes as a practical spiritual guide for the most pressing issues of our time and for the most vital question of happiness. What seems to be original and fantastic is seen to be but a deeper, the deeper, aspect of reality, and in accord with the deepest longing of our hearts. Kreeft demonstrates agile philosophical acumen in using etymological, philosophical, historical, and theological means to clarify an area that makes or breaks the best of people.

John Haas's essay on "Christ the Redeemer of Culture" serves as a capstone to this volume by directly addressing the Christian difference in culture and science. Haas illustrates that the relationship between religion, culture, and science is rife with problems when they are presupposed, by their very natures, to be at odds with each other. However, such dominant presuppositions are indicative neither of faith nor of reason, but rather of certain secular and Protestant perspectives that are characterized as subjective, and at times irrational and legalistic. Haas argues that certain secular and Protestant views have permeated much of contemporary American discourse, so that opposition and dissent rather than transformation and integration seem to be the only intelligible metaphors for the relationship between culture and religion. Views on freedom and truth are a case in point. A Protestant view of the total depravity of humanity creates a fundamental distrust of the capacities to reason and to will and thus to know truth and to be conformed to it in free human action. External authority is also distrusted, since, in principle, human imperfection is doubled in human institutions, such as governmental or ecclesial bodies. These perspectives are not simply the fixed coordinates that guided certain sixteenth-century reformers, but they dominate the contemporary American media and academic reflections that present religion as voluntaristic and morally legalistic.

In contrast, Haas presents a Catholic vision that both predates and effectively responds to these approaches with nuanced confidence in human and divine reason and in the capacity to redeem culture by transforming it in intelligent and principled ways. Human wisdom and goodness—both personal and communal—can be nurtured, even in the midst of the effects of sin. Human laws and customs can be established or shaped by Gospel principles, even without achieving a definitive work. This recalls that the root of the word "culture," *cultus,* comes from the Latin for worship. A people's religious beliefs, or our "ultimate concern" as Protestant theologian Paul Tillich said, move a people in the building of culture and law. Ultimate religious beliefs serve as fixed coordinates of reference that shape culture differently according to their sources, whether they are communal and sapiential or subjectivist and legalistic. In a Catholic vision, natural science and bioethics need not oppose faith. Indeed, instead of a metaphor of a crossroads between science and faith, between politics and religion, Haas recalls Pope John Paul II's vision that emphasizes the compatibility between faith and reason, between science and religion. Catholic thinkers should not, because of popular oversimplifications and misrepresentations, feel forced to choose between God and science. God is the single source of all truth—revealed and scientific— each in its own proper form and finality. The only opposition is found in their human expressions. Thus, John Paul II repeatedly called for a new evangelization that is not just one of individuals, who need to be transformed to the mind of Christ, as says St. Paul (Rom 12:2). Indeed John Paul II called for a re-evangelization of culture as well, with the trust that truth is one and that practical reason and good will can creatively inscribe the principles of the Gospel in contemporary law, custom, verse, and cinema. This redeeming of culture takes intelligence and courage as well as simplicity and childlike trust, the model for which Jesus Christ preeminently offers.

one

Edmund D. Pellegrino, M.D.

MEDICINE AND MEDICAL EDUCATION

IN NEWMAN'S UNIVERSITY

Gentlemen, it will be your high office to be the links in your generation between religion and science.

John Cardinal Henry Newman, 1858

In these few words Newman epitomized what he considered the central reason for his inclusion of a medical school in the Catholic University of Ireland. They were uttered in 1858 in his last lecture to the students and faculty of his medical school shortly before his resignation as rector. Within the context of Newman's customary ambiguity,

---

The epigraph is from the lecture "Christianity and Medical Science," in *The Idea of a University,* introd. George N. Shuster (Garden City, N.Y.: Image Books, Doubleday, 1959), 463.

anxiety, and some disdain for the profession of medicine as the antithesis of a liberal education, these words are at once startling and challenging.

For all Catholic universities they pose a challenge that is yet to be adequately met. Yet their pertinence for today's encounter between the Catholic medical moral tradition and contemporary bioethics is unquestionable. Newman certainly could not have anticipated how advances in the life sciences have come to challenge our beliefs about the nature and destiny of man. The central moral question for medicine today is how to use our expanding knowledge of human biology wisely, well, and within ethical constraints that take man's spiritual destiny into account.

Newman's challenge was no mere rhetorical flourish. Throughout his public statements he worried over the hubris, narrowness, and power of science and medicine. For him to assign so critical a task to medicine within his lofty idea of a university deserves more attention than it has received.

This essay reflects on Newman's ideas about medicine and medical education within his broader "idea" of a university, on his prescience in anticipating the importance of Catholic physicians and scientists learned both in their faith and in science, and on the implications of Newman's vision for Catholic medical schools today.

Newman's University

A major impetus for Newman's willingness to undertake the arduous task of founding a university was his conviction that education without religion was illusory and incomplete. He wanted very much to integrate Catholic and modern culture.[1] He was also distressed by the turn in his time away from liberal to practical education in England's universities. He lamented the serious lack of opportunities for

1. George N. Shuster, "Introduction" in *The Idea of a University* (Garden City, N.Y.: Image Books, Doubleday, 1959).

university education for Irish youth. He wanted to remedy both deficiencies by an education based in human reason and at the same time responsive to ecclesiastical authority.[2]

The lasting fame and influence of Newman's university reside less in its actual accomplishments than in the eloquence of the vision of a university he set forth in his famous lectures now known under the collective titles "The Idea of a University" and "Lectures on University Subjects."[3] The first series of lectures was published in 1853, one year before instruction actually started. In effect, they were a brilliant series of educational promissory notes that Newman never fully delivered upon. Their influence within and beyond Catholic education has been extraordinary, primarily because of their impassioned, clear, and sophisticated description of liberal education as the distinguishing mission of a true university.

Newman's influence is all the more amazing when we consider the short life of the Catholic University of Ireland (1854–1908), and the fact that only a few of its projected faculties ever came into being or produced graduates. Moreover, Newman himself served as rector for only seven years and then intermittently. During his tenure he had to interrupt his presence in Ireland repeatedly to attend to affairs at his oratory in Birmingham. Newman's eloquence, however, captured a wide audience with its unparalleled evocation of the recurrent intellectual, moral, and spiritual issues that had troubled Western civilization since the Middle Ages.

Newman's central and unflagging "idea" was the indispensability and utility of a liberal education. The end of such an education was to discipline the intellect for its own sake and "not for some particular or accidental purpose, some specific trade or profession."[4] In this he opposed John Locke's insistence that the goals of education should be practical and remunerative. He argued particularly against professional or scientific education as the primary end of university education.

2. Ibid., 54.   3. The Idea of a University.
4. Ibid., 171.

His anxieties about professional education, often repeated in his lectures, did not, however, obscure his vision. Despite his misgivings, Newman could not accept professional education outside the university: "But out of a university, a lawyer or doctor is in danger of being absorbed and narrowed by his pursuit."[5] Instead he maintained that "a cultivated intellect because it is a good in itself brings with it a power and a grace to every work and occupation which it undertakes and enables us to be more useful to many others."[6]

Newman's anxieties and ambivalence, tinged perhaps with a little disdain for the professions, did not lead him to neglect their importance. He planned a law school and observatory, and even a university press. Even such specialized fields as these he felt could be rescued from their narrowness by the graces of a liberal education. Paradoxically, it was Newman's medical school that lasted longer than any other unit in his university. It achieved a measure of success even before letters, philosophy, or theology had attained any degree of maturity. Indeed, it seems that Newman reversed his negative opinion in his last lecture to the medical faculty and students, when he charged them with the critical responsibility of linking science and religion.

Just how Newman's medical school would, or could, have carried out his assignment and how it might have been reshaped by its contacts with the liberal arts as he conceived them we shall never know. As Dwight Culler has warned us, we must practice a certain caution in judging both the potentialities and accomplishments of Newman's university. "One must think of the Catholic University as a tiny, intimate community, a very pleasant one apparently, whose activity has neither the scope nor advanced character one associates with university learning."[7] This modest enterprise had then, and has now, an impact all the more remarkable for its small beginnings.

---

5. Ibid., 182.
6. Ibid., 183.
7. Dwight Culler, *The Imperial Intellect: A Study of Newman's Educational Ideal* (New Haven: Yale University Press, 1955), 156.

Newman's Medical School

Classically and liberally educated as he was, Newman had in mind a comprehensive university according to the medieval model, that is, one that embraced the liberal arts as foundational, and also propaedeutic, for the study of theology, medicine, and law. This was the formula then being followed at Louvain in Belgium, which established its new university in 1834, and which was clearly also intended to be the modern ideal for Catholic higher education.

Newman's intention seems to have been to begin with the school of arts, letters, and philosophy. This was logical since he placed liberal education at the heart of his university. It was therefore probably more serendipity than plan that moved Newman to establish his medical school so early in the life of his university. Just as he was beginning the faculty of letters, the Cecilia Street Medical School, one of five in Dublin, became available for sale. The proprietors of that troubled institution had planned to close it. The Catholic University of Ireland assumed ownership in 1853, "lock, stock and barrel." Medical classes were thus able to begin almost immediately.

Newman' s justification for this move was a combination of practical good sense and idealistic purpose. From the practical point of view Newman saw the importance of the "jump start" a functioning unit would give his university. It would "make a show," and "command respect" while the "real university" could grow "under their shadow."[8] It was also a way, he thought, of attracting students to the arts and humanities faculties.

On the more elevated side, Newman saw the medical school as away of redressing the dearth of Catholic lecturers in the five medical schools then active in Dublin. Of the forty-nine lecturers only two were Catholic, and of the practitioners only twelve Catholics were in

8. Newman, as quoted in Fergal McGrath, *Newman's University: Idea and Reality* (London: Longmans Green, 1951), 331.

any position of authority.[9] Clearly Dublin needed a better representation of Catholics in its medical profession.

Even more important for the overall objectives of his university was Newman's conviction that a medical school in a Catholic university would provide the means for engagement of the philosophical, ethical, and religious challenges of modern science. This latter aim was a central concern for Newman. To this end he intended that theological reflection should shape the Catholic physician's response to medical science, and conversely, he hoped that physicians could inform the theological enterprise with reference to advances in science.

Newman's medical school came into existence at a stirring time in science and medicine. Newman makes no mention of these events, but it is unlikely that someone so alert to the thought of his own times would be totally ignorant of them. For example, in 1851, Thomson had advanced the thermodynamic theory; in 1852, William Snow traced the London cholera epidemic to the village pump. In 1855, Addison described pernicious anemia; in 1856, the worm causative of schistosomiasis was identified. In 1858, three major medical advances were announced—Virchow put forth the revolutionary idea of cellular pathology, Kekule described the benzene ring that was to revolutionize organic chemistry, and Gray published the most influential book in gross anatomy in modern times. These events were climaxed by Wallace and Darwin's theory of evolution, a challenge to religion and Christianity ever since. The *Origin of Species* was published in 1859.

Clearly the times were propitious for the dialogue between science and religion. Newman's concerns about their relationship were obviously correct. The Church had indeed to respond to the questions these and similar discoveries presented to Christianity. Graduates of a Catholic university were needed who "will go into the wide world of science as specimens and patterns of a discipline which is at once Catholic and professional."[10] Just how crucial Newman saw this

9. Ibid., 327.   10. Newman, as quoted in McGrath, 370.

aim for a Catholic medical school we shall see further in this essay.

Interestingly, as if to underscore the need for the confrontation of the sciences and theology, 1858 was the year in which Bernadette of Lourdes experienced her visions of the Blessed Virgin. How could these miraculous events be reconciled with science? There was indeed a need for scientifically grounded Catholics to show in their lives and work how faith and reason complemented each other. Something better was required than St. George Mivart's failed attempt.[11] In the century and a half since Newman initiated his enterprise, the unprecedented expansion of science, physical and biological, has made the relationship of science and Christian faith an even sharper challenge than it was for Newman.

Newman's medical school outlived the university by many years, lasting until 1908, when it was taken over by the National University. The medical school was then the only fully chartered unit of the Catholic University of Ireland. Its graduates were beginning to take positions of leadership in Irish medicine. How much of the Catholic formation Newman had hoped for actually took hold is difficult to ascertain. In any case, that hope came to an end when the school became part of the National University.

Medical Education within the Idea of a University

Newman never lost his deep uneasiness about the professions, specialization, and research. He saw them in some ways as the very antithesis to his idea of the way the intellect should be disciplined in a university. Professions and specialized knowledge narrowed the intellect and the person. Yet he also recognized their tremendous power and influence in society. He knew full well that to banish them from his university was to impair its mission of cultural evangelization. The antidote for the vices of specialization he well recognized was the cul-

11. Janet Browne, *Charles Darwin: The Power of Place* (New York: Knopf, 2002).

tivation of the intellect for itself. Such an intellect would be equipped to place special knowledge within its proper but limited sphere.

Newman's major worry was to avoid the intoxication by power that specialized knowledge encourages and the dehumanization of the person it effects in those who possess it.[12] Only with a liberal education will the professional "know where his science stands" and "gain [. . .] a special largeness and illumination."[13] The professions had to be in the university if they were not to fall victim to the hubris of power. But they had to also imbibe the largeness of mind he saw in the liberal arts if the professions were not to throw the university itself off course. Newman sought mightily to avoid the horns of this dilemma of tension between the liberal education and the education of the professional.

Newman's ideas about medicine, and parenthetically about science generally, seemed to mature as he gained better acquaintance with medical education through his involvement in the operations of his own medical school. This maturation is in evidence in the three lectures that he delivered, two to his medical faculty and student body—one at the beginning of his rectorship and one at the end—and one to his faculty of science.

The first of these lectures was delivered in 1855, and was entitled "Christianity and Physical Science."[14] It was delivered before Newman's school of science had begun to function. Its faculty of theology was in a nascent state. The medical school was already in operation but just barely. Nonetheless, Newman chose to focus early on the relations between the knowledge of revelation and that of the physical sciences. The medical school faculty represented for him the kind of audience for whom the historical conflict between science and theology would have pertinence. He contrasted their methodologies and their apparent contradictions, which he saw as a serious challenge to Christianity.

12. Newman, 182–83.   13. Ibid., 182.
14. Ibid., 390–412.

Newman took the classical Catholic position that truth cannot be contrary to truth and that reconciliation between science and Christianity had to be effected.[15] The place for such a reconciliation was the Catholic university, where the liberal arts, theology, and rigorous science could engage in productive dialogue with each other. In that dialogue, he warned, however, that theology must not become too dependent on or submissive to the power of scientific knowledge. Here again Newman was prescient. Today non-Catholic and some Catholic theologians have succumbed to this temptation, losing nerve in the face of the powers of modern science. But neither science nor society is served well when science is without ethical constraints.

Newman tended to see medicine perhaps a little too narrowly as a physical science. Later he understood better its close relationship with the social sciences, humanities, and others. He had no way to know that the most acute challenges to theology would soon come from the life sciences. The seeds of these conflicts were being sown, however, in Newman's time. Indeed, during the short life of the Catholic University Gregor Mendel (1822–1884) was at work uncovering the first secrets of heredity, which had to wait until the end of the twentieth century to be explained in chemical and physical terms. Darwin's monumental challenge to cultural and religious traditions was just beginning to be debated.

Newman continued his cogitations on science and religion in another lecture, entitled "Christianity and Scientific Investigation," this time before the rudimentary faculty of science.[16] Here he turned more specifically to the potential conflict between the investigative spirit and theology, once more emphasizing the unity of truth. Newman wisely counseled patience with apparent conflicts between truths of science and religion. He especially advised avoidance of hasty judgments. He relied heavily on the concept of the university as "The Im-

15. Ibid., 405.
16. Ibid., 413–32, "Christianity and Scientific Investigation."

perial Intellect" under whose broad aegis all truths eventually would be reconciled.[17]

Of importance in this lecture was Newman's defense of scientific investigation against restrictions on the range of research. He recognized the differences in the capabilities and peculiarities of each science. He was careful to distinguish freedom in science from freedom in matters of faith. "Great minds need elbow room, not indeed in the domain of Faith but of thought."[18] All of this was consistent with the aim expressed in the Introduction to his lectures "on the idea of a University." There he held that ecclesiastical authority is "the appropriate guide for Catholics in matters of faith."[19] But he did not envision Church authority entering into matters that were not essentially theological or ecclesiastical.

Cardinal Newman's thoughts about scientific research were as troubled as his ideas of professionalization and specialization. At times he saw research as narrowing the intellect and challenging Christian faith. At other times he realized fully well that science, even in the nineteenth century, was a most powerful force in shaping culture and human life. Like John Paul II later, Newman saw the Church as an instrument of intellectual ministry that must be in dialogue with culture without sacrificing its spiritual or evangelical mission. In that ministry the Church needed Catholic universities that were intellectually vigorous, and faithful as well.

The intimations about religion and science that occupied Newman as rector of a Catholic university were of special significance for medicine then, as they are even more so now. His most powerful reiteration of these ideas and his direct challenge to medical education came in the last lecture, which he delivered to medical students and faculty in 1858, the year of his retirement from the rectorship.

In this lecture, Newman speaks directly of "Christianity and Med-

17. Ibid., 417.
19. Ibid., 54.

18. Ibid., 429.

ical Science."[20] He laments the few opportunities he has had to address that particular audience. He seems to be chastening himself for having missed the opportunity to deal more directly with the place of medicine in a university and the Church. He is unequivocal that his purpose is to talk about the "exact relation of your profession to the Catholic University itself and towards Catholicism generally."[21]

Newman assures his listeners that the university and its school of medicine are not set up for a secular purpose. His medical school has more to do than to provide opportunities for Irish students to enter medicine, important as this might be. He says too that he wishes to speak "authoritatively" about the principal duty of the medical profession to religion. This he proceeds to do, but not until he has once more expressed his deep uneasiness about the hubris of medicine. Thus, he warns his listeners about the erroneous presumption to which medicine is subject, "the illusion that the world could not go on without it,"[22] that health is the highest good of man,[23] that "what is true in his own science is at once lawful in practice,"[24] that things that are advisable in themselves are by that fact morally licit, that what is true in one science must be true in another,[25] that man is no different from other animals. All of this is "certain sophism of the intellect."[26]

Newman's response to this "sophism" is unequivocal. Health is not man's highest end, medicine is not the highest science, and all things are subject to the higher laws of morals and religion. The truths of Catholic and Christian teaching are repositories of truths of a higher order, required to constrain the interpretation of scientific fact as the final explanation of reality.[27] The teachings of a higher law are the restraints science needs if it is not to behave like a planet "broken loose from its celestial system."[28]

20. Ibid., 453–64.
21. Ibid., 453.
22. Ibid., 454.
23. Ibid., 456.
24. Ibid., 459.
25. Ibid., 456–57.
26. Ibid., 456.
27. Ibid.
28. Ibid., 463.

As this lecture comes to a close Newman does an abrupt turn about. He began with a restatement of his recurrent worries about professionalism, science, and medicine in particular. He ends with this extraordinary prediction and charge: "Gentlemen, it will be your high calling to be the links in your generation between religion and science. Return thanks to the Author of all good that he has chosen you for this work."[29] In these few words Newman assigns to his medical school what he believed was a critical function of the university itself. Newman thus reaffirms his staunch belief that there is only one truth, that it cannot be known fully or reconciled in its apparent contradictions without continuing engagement of one view with the other. He has chosen medicine for this task of reconciliation fully, conscious of its dangers but also of its potentialities as a discipline that more than any other encounters man in all his dimensions—physical, social, humanistic, and spiritual. Clearly in this last lecture Newman has assigned to medicine in a Catholic university the central challenge of his times and of the university itself. He never defined in detail how this was to be done. But that it must be done is more certain today than it ever was in Newman's time. In the century and a half since the challenge was issued, how have Catholic medical schools responded?

Newman's Challenge Today

The challenge Newman issued to his medical school in his last lecture before its faculty was far more prescient than even he could have appreciated. Today the challenge to religion, and Christianity in particular, comes from the life sciences. Physics had put the origins of the universe in doubt. Biology today puts the origin, meaning, and purpose of man in doubt. Man now can reproduce himself without sexual intercourse, the possibility for cloning his own likeness is within reach, correction of errors in his genetic endowments is attainable,

29. Ibid.

enhancement of his capabilities is within sight, and even creation of simpler forms of life is theoretically possible. Biology is the new salvation theme of modem man, promising long life, bodily immortality, and control of the future of his own species.

The practical vehicle for these putative wonders is now medicine. As the concepts of health and disease become stretched, the range of what is "medical" stretches accordingly. Medicine as the pathway from the biological laboratory to everyday life is for many the means of liberation from religion, from "antiquated" concepts of morality, and of freedom to design ourselves and our children as we see fit. Even some who profess Christianity seem willing to compromise traditional morals and beliefs for the utilitarian benefits of applied biology.

Is Newman's hope that medicine would be the link bringing religion and science together altogether too fanciful? Is it asking more than medicine could possibly deliver? What would it mean in a Catholic university today?

I want to argue that Newman's vision of medical education within the borders of the university as he perceived it is exactly on target. If a Catholic university today is to fulfill Newman's idea of its mission in modem culture it can do so completely only if it includes a medical school. That medical school must of course then see itself as Newman did, as the link between science and Christianity. This is not to discredit universities without medical schools, but to reaffirm Newman's somewhat reluctant, but secure, belief that medical schools do belong in a university designed along the lines of his seminal idea of a university.

If the hubris of medicine that Newman rightly feared is to be modulated, medical schools must be in genuine dialogue with theology and philosophy. Medicine's image of man must be endowed with dignity because man is in fact the image of God. Medical ethics ultimately must therefore be grounded in a sound philosophical and theological anthropology. Such an image of man cannot be derived solely from the biological and physical phenomena of human life.

John Paul II in his encyclical *Ex Corde Ecclesiae* has brilliantly defined what it takes to make a university Catholic today.[30] In *Fides et Ratio, Veritatis Splendor,* and *Evangelium Vitae,* he has provided the intellectual substance essential to sustain a true Catholic university. Avery Dulles has recently very concisely pinpointed the advantages of a Catholic university.[31] The blueprints of an updated concept for Newman's idea are at hand.

What would it take if Catholic medical schools today were to respond to Newman's challenge within the framework both of his idea and of John Paul II's vision of the modem Catholic university? First, Catholic universities would need the moral courage to be different in a climate of academic correctness. Today, this "correctness" is equated with moral neutrality on the human life issues, freedom from all religious influence in the classroom, and fidelity to a bioethics based in the ideas of political liberalism, that is, freedom of choice, utilitarianism, moral diversity, and skepticism. Deviations from this ideological template usually incur charges by official academia of fettered intellects, inferior scholarship and science, and medieval obscurantism. These are formidable challenges. To yield is for Catholic medical schools to abrogate the reasons for their existence within the larger mission of the Catholic university.

Teaching bioethics in the framework of the Catholic tradition does not make Catholic universities into seminaries or convents. Their aim instead is to prepare physicians who understand when and how to confront the inevitable ethical choices that are part of modem medical practice. Their aim is not primarily moral and spiritual guidance, healing, and helping the sick within the requirements of respect for the dignity of every human being. The inviolability of the dignity of all— sick as well as healthy, poor as well as rich, young as well as old—is rooted in the scriptural identity of man in the image of God.

Professional formation, therefore, is as important as profession-

---

30. Pope John Paul II, *Ex Corde Ecclesiae* (Apostolic Constitution on Catholic Universities, August 15, 1990).

31. Avery Dunes, S.J., "The Advantages of a Catholic University," *America,* May 20, 2002: 19–21.

al information. What it is to be a Catholic and Christian physician requires the kind of interaction of science and religion Newman so clearly espoused. In this respect a heavy responsibility rests with the clinical teachers, the administration of the university hospital, and medical leadership to exhibit the Christian virtues in their daily contacts with students.

Second, if they are to educate the intellect for itself as Newman proposed, Catholic universities must rescue the liberal arts from their own narrowness. The humanities today are specialized fields of study. In few universities are the liberal arts taught as propaedeutic for all other studies as well as for their own sake. The idea of the liberal arts as education of the intellect in Newman's sense has been lost. Catholic medical students who are to be the links between Christianity and science must begin preparation for that task in college. They can do so only with a core curriculum in the liberal arts genuinely dedicated to education of the intellect for itself.[32]

Third, the premedical exposure to philosophy and theology must be more systematic, rigorous, and thorough than it is today. Given the complexity of the ethical issues vexing bioethicists today, Catholics need a sound grounding in the moral theology relevant to the Catholic tradition in medical morals. Personal experience teaching Catholic medical students in Catholic and non-Catholic universities reveals a discouraging dearth of information about the rudiments of the Faith. Moral theology is terra incognita for most Catholic college students.

Fourth, the sciences must of course be taught with rigor, with emphasis on those aspects fundamental to a comprehension of the life sciences at the cellular and molecular level. To strengthen the liberal arts component of medical education does not imply dilution of the scientific. Rather it emphasizes the integration of multifaceted dimensions of body, soul, mind, and psyche. Medicine is a humane science and a scientific humanism, incomplete without reference to man's spiritual nature.

32. E. D. Pellegrino, "Educating the Humanist Physician: An Ancient Ideal Reconsidered," *Journal of the American Medical Association* 227, no. 11 (March 1974): 1288–91.

Fifth, all points of view will need to be examined, whether they agree or not with official teaching. Medical students cannot be "links" without understanding the articulations between Catholic and non-Catholic points of view. Only then can the points of conjunction and disjunction between Catholic tradition, contemporary teaching, and postmodern ideas be unraveled. All of this requires an approach based in natural law, the dignity of man, and the way modern science challenges these notions.[33]

Sixth, so far as bioethics is concerned, there must be recognition of its importance and influence in public opinion and legislation. Catholic medical students must be amply prepared in both secular and Christian bioethics; bioethics is the arena in which today the confrontation of science and Christianity that Newman foresaw is taking place. Some critical mass of Catholics educated in bioethics will need to be specifically prepared for research, study, and dialogue in this crucial field. What we will need in effect is an apologetics of Christian bioethics.

But the task cannot be assigned to a new class of specialists and forgotten by the majority of physicians. Every Catholic physician is called upon to know the teachings of the Church, to apply them in his own practice, and to defend and explain them to patients and in public discourse. This will require a far more systematic and in-depth instruction in medical school in the Catholic medical moral tradition. The complex bioethical issues cannot be relegated to experts alone. Every physician will become the vehicle for the application of new and sometimes ethically questionable biology in his practice. Ethical decision making is as crucial to being a good clinician as good science. Practical skill in ethical decision making is becoming a professional requirement.

So far as bioethics goes, both secular and Catholic Christian formulations must be taught. Catholic physicians need to know what precisely bioethicists are teaching and how it impinges on their own

33. E. D. Pellegrino, "Bioethics at Century's Turn: Can Normative Ethics Be Retrieved?" *Journal of Medicine and Philosophy* 25, no. 6 (December 2000): 655–75.

faith commitments. They must be prepared to take human reason as far as it can go, since arguments based solely in scriptural or ecclesiastical authority will be discredited. Catholic physicians will need to practice a form of bioethical apologetics to make the Catholic Christian stance on such issues as cloning, stem cell research, genetic enhancement, and reproductive technology visible and convincing.

If Christian bioethics is to possess any degree of verisimilitude it must be exhibited in the care of patients. It follows then, that Catholic medical schools cannot satisfy Newman's challenge completely unless they also operate a hospital. There the principles of Catholic professional ethics and bioethics can serve as models of what being a Catholic healer actually means. It is there that the philosophical and theological principles emphasized in college and medical school can be brought to bear on daily decision making.

I will not go further into the details of medical education and patient care tailored to fit the requirements of Catholic and Christian bioethics. What is at issue here is a clear, unapologetic teaching and practice, uniting faith and reason, and engaging secular medicine on the highest academic and intellectual terms. If Catholic medical schools are to justify their separate existence then they should bring to education and care the example of Christian learning as well as charitable healing in a Christian apostolate of health care.

There are significant obstacles to this kind of response to Cardinal Newman's challenge, among Catholics and Catholic medical educators as well as non-Catholics.

Among Catholics, some will say pointedly that a distinctively Catholic stance will create an educational ghetto, dilute intellectual inquiry and scientific research, take students' valuable time away from medical subjects, or invite ecclesiastical interference. Others will confuse dialogue with accommodation to secular mores or to the opinions of "reasonable people." Still others will consider "under Catholic auspices" a sufficient commitment without being too specific about what that rubric means. Other Catholics will insist that the best medical students and faculties will eschew any appointment at a school so avowedly "Catholic."

Secularists will make the same objections but with much greater self-assurance. For them, religion, theology, and philosophy have no place in a scientific education. Any restriction on what is societally acceptable practice or on what is legally or scientifically permissible is a restriction on academic freedom. A hospital and physicians caring for patients in a pluralistic society must be "value neutral." They must provide a "full range" of socially condoned treatments irrespective of religious belief of the provider. A core curriculum, and especially one that requires philosophy and theology of an identifiable kind, is sure to distort a "liberal" education.

These are familiar objections. This is not the place for a detailed rebuttal. Newman's challenge is admittedly a difficult one, but one that somehow must be met. In the long run, universities must be judged as universities for their academic excellence. This need does not mean submission to the predominant ideological correctness of secular academia today. It does mean scholarship of the highest order, faculty and students of the highest quality, and willingness to engage in a dialogue with modem culture. To enter this dialogue from a clear and unambiguous stance based in the Catholic moral and intellectual tradition does not prohibit intellectual discourse.

Being Catholic need not relegate a university to lesser status. In the long run, faculty and students will gravitate to universities that cultivate the intellect for its own sake. That cultivation, Newman argued, can occur only within a truly Catholic environment.

Summary

Cardinal Newman's idea of a university has become a Magna Carta for Catholic higher education. Within that vision medicine, and parenthetically the other professional faculties, were given cautious place. Newman never relinquished his anxieties about their hubris and narrowness. But he also knew very well that excluding them from his idea of a university would be disastrous for physicians as for society.

Medicine is the profession with which he gained the most experience. What he thought about its educational goals is especially pertinent today. His prescience in anticipating the importance of Catholic thought in the era of modem bioethics is remarkable. His challenge to be the "link" between Christianity and science is far more urgent than it was in his time. It is a challenge Catholic medical schools worldwide have yet to adequately meet. I would venture to say that the justification for a Catholic medical school within a Catholic university will depend largely, if not solely, on how well it meets Newman's challenge.

That challenge is now nearly two hundred years old and more urgent than Newman could have imagined. In that time the life sciences have expanded their control of both life and death prodigiously. Unrestrained by an idea of man that takes account of his spiritual destiny, they can easily become the "death" sciences.[34]

Catholic physicians can be the links between religion and science only if their education is shaped by the worth and dignity of every human being. They must recognize that the impenetrability of the mystery of man will persist no matter how deeply science probes his physical reality.[35] This is the purpose of medical education within the "idea" of Newman's university, which has yet to be adequately attained. It is the only antidote to the medical sophism Newman so strongly repudiated.

34. Pope John Paul II, *Evangelium Vitae* (Encyclical Letter on the Value and Inviolability of Human Life, March 25, 1995).

35. E. D. Pellegrino, "What Is Man? The Mystery behind the Genome," in *What Is Man, O Lord? The Human Persona in a Biotech Age,* Proceedings of the Eighteenth Workshop for Bishops, ed. Edward A. Furton and Louise A. Mitchell (Boston: National Catholic Bioethics Center, 2002), 31–48.

two

⁀

Kevin L. Flannery, S.J.

TWO WINGS   *Aquinas and Aristotle*

In the first sentence of *Fides et Ratio,* John Paul II says that "Faith and Reason are like two wings on which the human spirit rises to the contemplation of truth." Both are necessary in order to fulfill the mission of the Church, and neither excludes the other; yet each is also justifiably jealous of its own methods and subject matter. The consequences of not using one or the other wing are obviously undesirable: the Church must both present the Faith and present it reasonably. But the consequences of confounding and/or confusing the two can be equally disastrous, although the basic error, being more subtle, often goes undetected or unremarked. It sometimes even passes for piety. I shall be more concerned here, therefore, with distinguishing than with uniting, although I would also insist that the distinguishing makes the unity possible. Single wings on separate birds are useless for flight; a single bird flies due to the balance of force between the wings it unites in itself.

There is no thinker in the history of the Church who better embodies the art of attaining balance in distinction than Thomas Aquinas, and his desire to find the point of reasoned equilibrium between theology and philosophy is very much in evidence in his thinking about the temporal creation of the world (the universe); so, I would like to begin with that. Thomas's discussion of temporal creation largely concerns Aristotle's doctrine that the world is eternal. Later on I shall discuss Thomas's use of Aristotle—who represented for him philosophy itself—in some theological contexts. This, I hope, will give us more insight into the relationship between philosophy and theology.

One of Thomas's earliest—and most important—writings on creation in time is article five of the first question (and distinction) of the second book of the commentary on Peter Lombard's *Sentences*. Thomas very often begins his treatment of an issue by first raising objections to his own position, then setting out that position, followed by specific responses to the objections. But in this article he, in effect, includes a second set of objections taking a line opposite to that of the original set, but also different from his own position. That is, the first set of objections argues that Aristotle was right: the world is eternal; the second set (representing a number of Christian authors) argues that Aristotle was *demonstrably* wrong. Thomas answers each set of objections individually, as well as staking out his own middle ground between the two camps.

Thomas, of course, ultimately agrees with the Christian position. To say that the world is eternal contradicts the first line of the Bible: "In the beginning God created heaven and earth." But he does not think that this can be known independently of divine revelation. He was, indeed, embarrassed by the way his fellow believers strove to confute the philosophers who held for the world's eternity, deploring the weakness of their arguments. Such arguments, he says, "result more in derision than in confirmation of the Faith."

Actually, I think that Thomas is being a bit rough on his fellow

Christians here. Any attempted proof of a proposition, if it is to have respectability as a proof at all, must proceed logically; it must not employ fallacious arguments or specious syllogisms. Such a proof can sustain a false conclusion if one of the premises from which it follows is false. The way then to ensure that one's conclusions are true is (obviously) to make sure that all one's premises are true. But ensuring that the premises are true is especially difficult when the argument bears upon issues such as the creation of the world. The premises of arguments bearing upon issues close to us are relatively easy to support: often we can simply check the facts to see whether they correspond to the premises. As our questions verge, however, toward the boundaries of reason itself, we are forced to tread more tentatively. An argument about the creation of the world, of course, says something about concrete events in the world about us; but it also bears us away from their immediate causes to the causes of these, then to the causes of these latter, and so on, until we reach the first cause (or causes) in the series. At this extreme, we can only just "feel our way." We cannot expect to find there objects hitting other objects with the familiar predictable results or even to find our trusted methods of analysis to be working as usual.

Thomas himself relays a delightful little vignette, taken from the Jewish philosopher Moses Maimonides, in order to depict this state of affairs. Maimonides tells the story of a boy raised on a desert island, away from his parents and mankind in general. He is found and reintroduced into society, learning to speak, and so on; one day he is told that humans such as himself spend nine months in the wombs of their mothers. He objects that this could not be, since a man cannot live without breathing and eating and expelling waste (!)—and how could this continue for months in the womb?

Maimonides's (and Thomas's) point is that the problem with so many arguments regarding the beginnings of the universe is that we can hardly resist our habitual—even natural—inclination to explain such an event to ourselves in the terms we use to explain all other events. For instance, individual events in the world as we normally consider it cannot be grasped at all unless we understand two things: when they begin and when they finish. But beginnings are different from what they begin in at least one important way: it makes no sense at all to talk about when a *beginning* finished. Thus, when we seek to understand creation, one of the very prerequisites of our normal understanding is excluded. We lack a foothold and are easily thrown off balance. It is no surprise, therefore, and no great shame, that many Christian thinkers in Thomas's time slipped and stumbled when it came to theorizing about the creation of the world.

Let us take now a closer look at the article, already mentioned, from Thomas's commentary on the *Sentences*. I will consider the sets of objections in order, in each case examining just one of the arguments presented (each being an argument in which the Aristotelian position is immediately at issue). So then, in the first set, in favor of the eternity of the world, we find an argument in which Aristotle says that all that is real of time is the present moment, which he defines, reasonably enough, as the end of the past and the beginning of the future. But if the present moment is always preceded by a past moment, that past moment, when it was present, was preceded by a different past moment, and so on; therefore time, which belongs to the world, goes back with the world eternally.

Thomas's reply to Aristotle—and, remember, we are talking about *the* Philosopher here, so in a sense we are talking about philosophy itself—is that he does not demonstrate his case. Aristotle's concept of time, notes Thomas, is tied up with his concept of motion since time is the number (or the measure) of motion. Motion, of course, is itself tied up with matter, since only material things move. To say, therefore, that before the present moment (which corresponds to a motion) there was another moment (which also corresponded to a motion), is to begin with the proposition that was to be proved: that is, that before any given moment (and motion), another moment (and motion) can always be found in existence. Aristotle was steeped in the ancient methods of dialectical argumentation, in which two individuals engage in philosophical disputation, the one trying to undermine the position of the other. In such a disputation, the first interlocutor, in effect, asks the other, "Will you accept *p?*" If yes, the game begins. But the second interlocutor will not accept *p* if it is too close to what the first interlocutor has to prove. He can always cry, *"Petitio principii!"* or "You have begged the question!" In the present instance, the first interlocutor asks for agreement to the proposition, "before the present moment, there was a previous moment (which this one finishes)." But this is too close to what has to be proved: he has begged the question.

As I have already said, things of this sort inevitably happen when an argument gets pushed to the edges of reason itself—which is to say, to the ends of reasons for holding positions. In most arguments, you gain ground on your adversary by identifying "higher" reasons (or principles) with which he also agrees, and then showing that your position follows from those principles and his does not. The distance between the higher principles and the matter at hand provides a sort of leverage, by means of which you hope to bring your adversary over to your point of view. But when arguments come down to the very natures of things, especially things such as time and motion, they inevitably turn on definitions, which *are* principles, or, at least, are very close to them. Definitions are formulated in order to gain consensus, so, at least at the beginning of the investigation, the usual argumentative leverage seems unattainable.

In the cases at hand, we can, however, gain a foothold by attending to the relationship between definitions and reality. A definition is good to the extent that it corresponds to what the thing to be defined *is*. What time and motion are, is given to us: they do not depend upon our definitions of them. Our definitions of them cannot, therefore, take us beyond what we are given of them. Imagine that you are the one and only human being in the world. You are set down in the world at a particular time and will go out of it at a particular time. Your task while you are there (or here) is to compose good definitions of what you experience, including time, based on what you come to know of it. Because the things you find in the world do not depend upon your definitions but, rather, the accuracy of your definitions depends on the things you find, you are never on safe ground if ever your definition takes you beyond the natures (the things) set before you. If your definition of time—rather than time itself—implies that time existed before you arrived, it may very well be pointing to something true, but you have no way of proving this: no reason to believe it. An argument based only on that definition and intended to prove that the world existed before you arrived would not be conclusive. This is not to say, of course, that you would not have reason to believe that the world did exist before you arrived, but only that such a proof cannot depend on one of your definitions.

This is Thomas's point in his criticism of Aristotle's argument for the eternity of time. That argument depends directly upon the definition of the present moment that Aristotle proposes: "the end of the past, the beginning of the future." Although this definition is intuitively plausible, *it* cannot be used to determine anything about the nature of time itself (or the present moment) since the task of a definer is to match definitions to reality, not the other way around. Forced to extremes such as those involved in the consideration of creation, an interlocutor can always insist on being given a definition that does not beg the question at issue. He can insist, for instance, on defining the present moment in this way: "The present moment is the end of the past and the beginning of the future—unless it is the very first or the very last moment, in which two cases it is just the beginning of the future or just the end of the past, respectively." This new definition is more of a mouthful, of course, but at least it does not beg the question.

Let us look now at an argument put forward by at least some Christians of Thomas's time as a refutation of Aristotle. Thomas directs a very similar counterargument against them. Some who know the truth that the world is not eternal argue, for instance, that if it were eternal we could never arrive at the present day. Cast your mind back on a supposed infinite number of former days. If there is no beginning of them, we have no firm first day, from which we might begin to count forward in order to arrive at the present day. Therefore, or so the argument goes, the world cannot be eternal. But, as with the Aristotelian arguments for the eternity of the world, this argument smuggles in that which it is meant to prove. When the defender of the Faith asks us to cast our minds back on a supposed infinity of days, suggesting that we can find in such a conception no solid basis from which to begin counting, he is simply presupposing the contrary of what Aristotle asserts: that is, that there is *always* such a solid basis, since the world always exists. And this is an illegitimate argumentative move: it gets us nowhere.

Think of the world as being here now. There is nothing illogical in thinking of it as existing also yesterday, and the day before, and so on for an infinity of time. The world, understood thus, would simply always be *here*. To say that in order to count forward to the present time we need an absolutely first day is to insist that all counting correspond to the common type of counting, in which one begins with the first in a series (of pages, for instance) and finishes with the last. But it is perfectly possible to count off in other circumstances.

Assume that we do not know whether the world is eternal or not. Independently of whether it is or not, we can still have information regarding an event in the past: it could be an event toward the beginning of all memory—the flooding of Atlantis, for instance, mentioned by Plato—or a more recent event, such as the birth of Christ. Given any such a foothold, we can begin counting days, hours, or minutes in either direction. Indeed, in dealing with the duration of the universe, since we were not *there* at its beginning, we are necessarily in this very situation of having to make do with whatever foothold is available. But given this situation, the believer in a finite world cannot refute the philosopher who thinks that the world is eternal.

Imagine the believer and the pagan philosopher both considering the same span of time: the time between the birth and the death of Socrates, for instance. There is nothing in that span of time that entails that it does—or does not—have an infinite number of real predecessors. Logic will not take us back to the beginning of time; its task is rather to help us organize the things that we already know by other means: to determine what follows from what, what is contradictory, and the like.

What does all this tell us, then, about the relationship between philosophy and theology, the two wings of the Christian intellectual's life? John Finnis once recounted to me a remark made by Joseph de Finance, S.J., after a lecture. Having spoken about the relationship between philosophy and theology (or sacred doctrine) in such a way as vindicated especially the role of philosophy, de Finance was asked, Well, then, what's the *use* of theology? What does it give us that philosophy does not? His answer was as simple as it was profound. "It gives us more information."

I have been insisting that definitions are answerable to reality (not reality to them). Now, it is not by chance that some of the most powerful attempts to prove that the world is eternal turn on definitions. A definition is the precise formulation of information that stands before the definer; and that there was a moment when the world was created is information. Thus, a definition is the *sort* of thing one needs to get into one's argument if one's conclusion is to say something about the temporal origin of the world. But no human definer was present at the moment of creation. If, therefore, we are to know something about the origin of the world, the information must come to us from someone else, whose testimony we believe. And we do have such information. In sacred Scripture, properly interpreted, God tells us that the world had a temporal origin. Here we see clearly the relationship between philosophy and theology. Theology, which has as its principles the truths of revelation, expands the information presented to the human mind: that is, to philosophy (and to the other human disciplines). Philosophy is incapable on its own of generating such information; but, once it has accepted such information as true, it can—and inevitably will—work with it, studying its meaning and implications, as it does with respect to any information.

This all helps us to understand some of the claims that Thomas makes with respect to his pagan master Aristotle. Take, for instance, his attribution to Aristotle of a doctrine of creation. Yes, creation. Not creation in *time,* knowledge of which comes by way of revelation, but the dependence of all things upon God for their very being. This is something we can come to know just by considering the things we find in the world and reasoning about them. The proof depends not on illegitimate definitions that reach beyond what is warranted but on good definitions and a proper understanding of the metaphysical structure of the things to which they refer.

Any advance in understanding (or intelligibility) is an advance in dignity and importance within the causal structure of the world. Forms are more intelligible than matter is. As we go toward matter, there is less intelligibility; as we go toward form, there is more. For instance, there is more intelligibility in a dog than in the matter—the flesh and bones—of which it is formed, if only because higher forms such as dogs encompass lower forms such as calcium, sodium, phosphorous, and the like, which *contribute* to the nature of dogs. Something's intelligibility implies an intellect—that is, a center of intelligibility—independent of the intelligibility of the thing itself, since a thing cannot give to itself its own entire intelligibility. We can, for instance, set in order parts of ourselves—we can repair limbs and organs so that our whole organism might function as it should, or we can bring under rational control our thoughts and emotions—but we cannot give to our nature itself its own intelligibility (or form). That comes from something higher: and, since higher here means "more intelligible," that something higher must be an intellect of some sort.

By arguing along these lines, philosophy, independently of theology, is capable of demonstrating that the world depends on God for its very being—and this is for God to be "creator," at least according to a certain sense of that word. The thing that philosophy cannot demonstrate, according to Thomas, is whether or not there was a moment when God gave this being, in all its intelligibility, to the world. It cannot do this because philosophy is part of that creation. Even if it were true that in the first moment of the world's existence there existed a philosopher, how would he prove that *that* moment was the first? Again, we can suppose that he sets about the task of defining—an essential task for a philosopher—and, in particular, that he wishes to define "time." As we have seen, he cannot legitimately go beyond time as he experiences it. Even if the first moment that he knows is the first moment of the world's existence, there is nothing in that moment that says anything about whether it is first or not. That the world was created in time is known only by God—and by those with whom he has shared the information and who accept it as true.

Or let us take another faith-associated idea that Thomas attributes to Aristotle—and, indeed, one even more surprising than creation since it is even more naturally regarded as connected with revelation: grace. Near the end of his *Eudemian Ethics,* Aristotle discusses the phenomenon of people who perform good actions and live good and noble lives but are not in possession of practical wisdom. They are "good people," but they would not be able to explain in a precise manner how they arrive at their decisions to perform good actions. They constitute a philosophical problem for Aristotle since, at least at first sight, according to his own theory, it is practical wisdom that *produces* such characteristics. In the end, Aristotle settles on the following explanation of how this works: such a person strikes upon right and beneficial actions because there are present in his soul "impulses" that are ordered toward good things.

How do we explain the presence of these impulses? Aristotle's reply, in fact, is not unrelated to his ideas about God as the ultimate cause (the creator) of the world. It is true that in analyzing what a person does we can often link one decision to another: the decision to call a taxi might depend upon a decision to go home for lunch, for instance. But eventually the series must come to a stop. Where does it stop, asks Aristotle? With God. "That which is sought is this [says Aristotle]: What is the source of motion in the soul? The answer is clear: as in the universe it is God, so also here. For in a sense the divine in us moves everything. The source of reason is not reason but something greater."

This Aristotelian passage is cited several times by Thomas Aquinas, in some very theological contexts. (The passage is part of a work that circulated in medieval times under the title *De bona fortuna.*) In a passage in the *Summa theologiae* (Ia-IIae, q. 68, a. 1.), for instance, he expounds Isaiah 11:2: "And upon him will rest the spirit of wisdom and understanding," and so on—that is, the classic text for the gifts of the Holy Spirit. This scriptural text, he explains, is about inspiration, which comes to us from outside human reasoning. And, although the gifts of the Holy Spirit are very clearly *super*natural gifts, that is, beyond the natural capacities of man, Thomas uses as an authority Aristotle. There is a "double moving principle" in man, he says: one interior, which is reason, another exterior, which is God. And then he cites in favor of this position the passage from the *Eudemian Ethics* that we have just seen.

A similar argument is found in Thomas's "Against the teaching of those discouraging religion." In this small work, written just three years before his death, Thomas opposes those who would discourage vocations to the religious life. So, again, the topic is grace—and, in particular, the grace that moves the soul directly, by means of holy impulses. In Thomas's time, there were, apparently, people who denied the divine origin of such impulses. Thomas cites against them both sacred Scripture and the Church Fathers; and then he discusses the chapter of the *Eudemian Ethics* we have been looking at. He mentions first the idea we have already seen, that the source of reason is greater than reason itself, and then quotes Aristotle to the effect that it makes no sense to offer counsel to individuals blessed with supernatural impulses since their thoughts and choices are initiated by God. "Someone who calls himself Catholic ought, therefore, to be embarrassed," says Thomas, "referring the divinely inspired to human counsels, of which a pagan philosopher asserts they have no need."

So then, to return to *Fides et Ratio* and to conclude, these are both very useful passages for attaining clarity about the relationship between the "two wings on which the human spirit rises to the contemplation of truth." For they force upon us a number of questions that go right to the heart of the matter. What did Aristotle—the Philosopher—know? How did he know it? And what did he *not* know? It is clear that, according to Thomas, Aristotle knew about supernatural grace. He came to know about it, presumably, by looking around him and by considering Greek culture more generally and realizing that there were individuals in that culture whose behavior could be explained only by positing the influence of supernatural grace. Obviously, these individuals were not Christians, and they are unlikely to have had any contact with Jewish culture; so the grace involved would not have arrived by the "ordinary channels." And neither would it have been something merely analogous to the grace that operates upon Jews and Christians. It must have been the real thing, since Thomas cites Aristotle as support for what he says about the grace operative in Jewish and Christian hearts.

But if Aristotle knew about supernatural grace, what did he lack? If even a pagan philosopher can know about grace, what is left to the theologian? The answer depends on the same idea that came to the fore when we considered creation: the idea of *information*. Both Aristotle and a number of Christian philosophers erred by failing to understand that knowledge of the time of creation is a piece of information and not a conclusion generated by and within philosophy itself. Similarly, although on purely philosophical grounds Aristotle was able to arrive at the idea of grace, he lacked the information that grace comes to men—to righteous gentiles and to Jews, whether they know it or not—through Jesus Christ. This is "what is left to the theologian," to be expounded and preached, making use of whatever means are available, philosophical or theological, natural or supernatural.

The information that grace comes through Jesus Christ is no mean information. Because we have heard it so often, we tend to take it for granted. But let us think about what it is and what it implies. The information that grace comes through Jesus Christ implies that it comes to us through a Jew, born some two thousand years ago. This, in turn, is tied up with the truth that the creator of the world speaks to us in Jewish holy Scriptures—and also in the Christian Scriptures, which continue and complete the former. And this, when combined with the truth that God does not lie, implies that the same God-become-man founded a Church, investing it with his own authority and infallibility. Aristotle would have rejoiced to have such information. But it would have been precisely that: information, divine information, and not part of his philosophy.

three

Jude P. Dougherty

WRETCHED ARISTOTLE

"Wretched Aristotle!" The words are those of Tertullian (c. 160–c. 220), better known perhaps for his rhetorical question, "What does Athens have to do with Jerusalem?" In Tertullian's words, "God has spoken to us: it is no longer necessary for us to philosophize. Revelation is all that is required. He who believes in the word of God knows more than the greatest philosophers have ever known concerning the only matter of vital importance."[1] Tertullian was not the first or the last to reject the use of classical learning in an attempt to understand the truths of the Gospels. Tatian, who preceded him by at least a generation, similarly rejected all efforts to employ Hellenistic learning in biblical exegesis or Christian apologetics. Centuries later, Luther, like his ancient pre-

---

1. As quoted by Etienne Gilson, *History of Christian Philosophy in the Middle Ages* (New York: Random House, 1954), 44.

decessors, was to rail against classical learning, particularly Aristotle, and the use made of Greek and Roman learning by the Scholastics. As he said, "Virtually the entire *Ethics* of Aristotle is the worst enemy of grace."[2] Reason is contrary to faith, Luther maintained, and it is impossible to harmonize the two. Modern versions of this notion are to be found in the anti-metaphysical and fideistic views of Kierkegaard and his twentieth-century disciples such as Karl Barth, Rudolf Bultmann, and Paul Tillich.

By contrast with Tatian and Tertullian, Justin Martyr and Clement of Alexandria used all the intellectual tools available to understand and defend the faith. Justin Martyr, a Greek who flourished in the mid-decades of the second century, brought to his apologetics a knowledge of Plato, Aristotle, Pythagoras, and the Stoics. He had read Plato's *Apology, Crito, Phaedrus,* and *Phaedo,* and other works that are still found on the reading lists of introductory courses in philosophy in those Catholic colleges that have remained true to their tradition. As a result of his study, Justin concluded that philosophy leads to Christianity as its fulfillment. The "rational" bequeathed by the Greeks is complemented by "revelation."[3] Pagan philosophy is not to be feared, for it is consistent with biblical teaching. Plato, he thought, was superior to the Stoics in knowledge of God, though inferior to them in ethics. The same esteem for portions of Greek philosophy came to be shared by Athanagoras, Theophilus of Antioch, Clement of Alexandria, and others.

Clement became so immersed in Greek philosophy that some regard him as more of a philosopher than the theologian he certainly was. Refusing to adopt the style of contemporary apologists, he took as his mission the straightforward teaching of the Faith to unbelievers. To that end he found philosophy indispensable. The Greeks had

2. As quoted by Jacques Maritain, *Three Reformers* (London: Sheed and Ward, 1950), 30. Maritain draws heavily on F. Ueberweg and M. Heinze, *Grundriss der Geschichte der Philosophie,* vol. 3 (Leipzig, 1914).

3. Cf. Gilson, *History of Christian Philosophy,* 11–14.

prepared the way for the reception of the truths of the Gospels, and Clement was convinced that Providence in directing historical events willed the existence of philosophers "because like a good shepherd, he wanted to put his best sheep at the head of his flock."[4] Jewish law and Greek philosophy, he maintained, are the two rivers at whose confluence Christianity has sprung forth. Sacred Scripture allows us to make use of profane learning without mistaking philosophical wisdom for the superior wisdom of Christianity. Since no one philosophical school possesses the whole truth, the first task of the Christian philosopher is to eliminate from philosophy all that is false. The only completely useless philosophical sect is that of Epicurus. With respect to the others, Christianity acts as a selective guide. Assuredly the doctrine of Christ is sufficient unto salvation, but philosophy can be used to lead men to Christ and further used to elucidate the teachings of Christ once they have been accepted.[5]

Origen of Alexandria (185–ca. 254), an Egyptian, is considered one of the great names in the history of Christian thought despite his many theological errors from an orthodox Christian viewpoint. A prolific writer, sometimes called a universal genius, he became a Christian biblical exegete worthy of translation by St. Jerome. Origen possessed an extensive knowledge of Greek philosophy—Aristotelian, Platonic, Stoic, and Epicurean. He adopted the basic elements of Plato's cosmology and psychology while borrowing his terminology and definitions from Aristotle. One of his students said of him, "He required us to study philosophy by reading all existing writings of the ancients, both philosophers and religious poets, taking care not to put aside or reject any . . . apart from the writings of atheists. . . . He selected everything that was true in each philosopher and set it before us, but condemned what was false."[6]

---

4. Cf. ibid., 32.

5. Cf. ibid., 29–34.

6. Gregory Thaumaturgus in *Origenem oratio,* quoted by M. L. Clarke, *Higher Education in the Ancient World* (London: Routledge and Kegan Paul, 1971), 126–27.

Eusebius of Caesarea similarly exploited the notion that the Greek philosophers and poets were providentially sent by God in preparation for the Gospel. That judgment has been echoed through the ages, most often expressed in the common dictum, "Christ came in the fullness of time when the intellect of the West was prepared to receive the truths of the Gospel." Without doubt the work of Justin, Clement, and Eusebius is echoed in the Scholasticism of the thirteenth century.

Nevertheless the dismissal of Greek learning and philosophy by Tatian and Tertullian did not pass away but remains today as the belief of a major sector of Protestantism. Luther, in keeping with his doctrine of Adam's fall and its debilitating effect on human intelligence, wrote, "Aristotle is to theology what darkness is to light." And further, "Aquinas [as a result of his indebtedness to Aristotle] . . . never understood a chapter of the Gospels."[7] It is impossible, he maintained, to reform the Church if Scholastic theology and philosophy are not torn out by the roots with Canon Law. In contrast to Clement, Luther claimed that "one should learn philosophy as one learns witchcraft, that is, to destroy it; that is, as one finds out about errors in order to refute them."[8]

Luther's disparagement of philosophical reason was to receive support in the eighteenth century from the British empiricists, who effectively undermined confidence in reason' s ability to move from the seen to the unseen. Kant confirmed the death of natural theology by his *First Critique,* and it has become commonplace in the dictum of William James that since Kant it is no longer necessary to consider proof for the existence of God. Enlightenment philosophy, in robbing faith of its rational preamble, led to the fresh examinations of the nature of religious belief. Perhaps the most notable leader of effort was Søren Kierkegaard.

In the long line of theologians stretching from Luther himself to Brunner, Barth, and Bultmann, Søren Kierkegaard holds a unique

7. As quoted by Jacques Maritain, *Three Reformers,* 30–31.
8. Ibid., 31.

place. He was the first to state, in more-or-less modern form, the case against the use of philosophy as a preamble to theology. Luther had stated it before him, but the rationalism Luther opposed was the comparatively modest rationalism of the Schoolman and Erasmus. What Kierkegaard had to contend with was the rationalism of Hegel. Drawing upon Kant in his attack on Hegel, he goes one step further, robbing religion, specifically Christianity, of any "objective" content. Faith, he declares, is not a matter of belief that can be set forth in propositional form, nor is religion a rational affair.[9]

Making a distinction between the world of universals (scientific generalizations) and the subjective world (inwardness), Kierkegaard asserted that whereas philosophy teaches us to become objective, Christianity teaches us to become subjective. Evidence for God's existence is an "objective question," but we find no conclusive evidence for His existence. Whether we can demonstrate the existence of God or not makes no difference from the standpoint of faith. Far more important is what happens to the individual when he is called upon to believe that which cannot be objectively known. With respect to objective matters, there will always be doubt, but what is important is what happens to the individual in the face of doubt. The believer is not turned away by objective uncertainty but instead passionately affirms. Kierkegaard calls this "subjective truth."

Subjective truth, we may note, is not truth in the usual sense; it is what is usually called "faith." For Kierkegaard, "Faith is precisely the contradiction between the infinite passion of the individual's inwardness and objective uncertainty. If I am capable of grasping God objectively, I am not believing, but precisely because I cannot so grasp God, I must believe. If I wish to preserve myself in faith, I must constantly be intent on holding fast the objective uncertainty, so as to remain out upon the deep, over seventy thousand fathoms of water, still

9. A primary text for Kierkegaard's doctrine of belief is *Either/Or,* 2 vols.; vol. 1 trans. David F. Swenson and Lillain Marvin Swenson; vol. 2 trans. Walter Lowrie (Princeton, N.J.: Princeton University Press, 1944).

preserving my faith."[10] The implications of Kierkegaard's thought are played out on the contemporary scene. Belief, of course, is a personal act, an act of assent to propositions acknowledged to be true, but the believer must somehow discern what is true. The Fathers of the Church who made the most of classical learning did so because what they had learned from Greek and Roman sources were truths that cohered with revelation, and furthermore by employing the categories of philosophical learning, they were better able to grasp the import of revelation.

In the realm of ideas, if reason is eschewed, everything is permitted, even where the Scriptures themselves are taken to be normative. In the aftermath of Vatican II, the Scholastic philosophy, which gave birth to the great medieval theological achievements and to the Thomistic movement of the nineteenth and early twentieth centuries, was scorned with Luther-like contempt by the "new theologians," who effectively removed it from the curricula of most Catholic colleges and seminaries. The result has led to ambiguity in theology, with consequences not only for traditional moral teaching but for our understanding of sacraments and even the Eucharist. In short, the church has been Protestantized in ways previously regarded as unthinkable.

This trend has been addressed by John Paul II. Echoing Clement of Alexandria, he opens his encyclical *Fides et Ratio* with this sentence: "Faith and reason are like two wings on which the human spirit rises to the contemplation of truth";[11] he asserts later, "I wish to repeat clearly that the study of philosophy is fundamental and indispensable to the structure of theological studies and to the formation of candidates for the priesthood." While the Church has no one philosophy over another, John Paul II, as Leo XIII before him, recommends the study of St. Thomas Aquinas as a model because "in his thinking, the

10. Søren Kierkegaard, *Concluding an Unscientific Postscript* [*Afsluttende Uvidenskabelig efterskrift* (1846)], trans. D. F. Swenson (Princeton, N.J.: Princeton University Press, 1941), 182.

11. John Paul II, *Fides et Ratio,* n. 62.

demands of reason and the power of faith found the most elevated synthesis ever attained by human thought."[12]

Strong words for those who succeeded in substituting second-order disciplines for the metaphysics of Aristotle and Aquinas. The fulfillment of John Paul II's admonition to return to old ways will not be easily accomplished. The great centers of learning that produced the scholars of a previous generation have long ago abandoned their heritage. In many, individual Catholic scholars steeped in the *philosophia perennis* are to be found, but the concerted efforts of a whole department are rare. This in spite of strong evidence that the young are eager for the type of learning that will enable them to escape the relativism and moral degeneracy of the age. The scholars among us who have maintained the learning of ancient Greece and Rome that shaped the Fathers and great commentators across the centuries are to cherished.

A clear Catholic voice is clearly needed. Writing in 1937 for an American audience, the Spanish-born Harvard University professor George Santayana observed:

> The present age is a critical one and interesting to live in. The civilization characteristic of Christendom has not disappeared, yet another civilization has begun to take its place. We still understand the value of religious faith. On the other hand, the shell of Christendom is broken. The unconquerable mind of the East, the pagan past, the industrial socialist future confront it with equal authority. On the whole life and mind is saturated with the slow upward flirtation of anew spirit—that of an emancipated, atheistic democracy.[13]

In the early decades of the last century, that judgment may have required the perceptiveness of a Santayana. Today it is almost universally accepted. Few are blind to the loss of a religious allegiance and its moral and cultural consequences. Santayana's assessment is echoed in a recent work by John M. Rist, emeritus professor of classics at the

12. Ibid., n. 78.

13. George Santayana, "Winds of Doctrine," in *The Works of George Santayana*, vol. 7 (New York: Scribners, 1937), 5.

University of Toronto. To give you an idea of his pedigree, his previous works bear such titles as *Plotinus: The Road to Reality, The Mind of Aristotle,* and *Augustine: Ancient Thought Baptized.* Writing some sixty-five years after Santayana, Rist, in a book newly released by Cambridge University Press entitled *Real Ethics,* but one that is not likely to be reviewed widely, assesses the damage foreseen by his celebrated predecessor.[14] Addressing what he calls the deception, equivocation, outright lying, and humbug that pass for contemporary moral discourse, humbug that extends from the universities into the marketplace, legislative assemblies, and juridical bodies, he offers a defense of traditional Christian morality grounded in classical metaphysics. In rather forceful language he writes that there is "no need to look in the public lavatory for the lowest common denominator."[15] The habits of what was lowlife morality have become the norms of moral and political discourse. "In the wake of any clear sense of what 'low life' might suggest, intellectuals are becoming 'downwardly mobile' and while losing their grip on an overall concept of virtue, often see such a direction as in itself virtuous and high minded, or sentimentally as solidarity with the marginalized or dispossessed."[16]

Despairing of any principled agreement on the foundations of morality between theist and nontheist, Rist takes a position reminiscent of Clement, who elected to preach the Gospel rather than to dialectically engage his contemporaries. In Rist's judgment upholders of the realist tradition must work through its history, learning from the skills and insights of those who advance it and from those who reject it. "Those who reject it must be forced to acknowledge their own Nietzschean parentage, a lineage that gives license to force and majeure, lies, hypocrisy, and intellectual dishonesty or triviality which make it palatable to a credulous and largely pre-philosophic public."[17] The realist tradition for Rist begins not with Aristotle but with Plato, a tra-

---

14. John M. Rist, *Real Ethics* (Cambridge: Cambridge University Press, 2002).
15. Ibid., 5.   16. Ibid., 6.
17. Ibid., 272.

dition unashamedly theological. Speaking to what he calls a crisis in the contemporary Western debate about ethical foundations,[18] he declares that Platonism and deception are the only moral and political alternatives available.

I have argued that if one is to engage one's contemporaries, one needs a philosophical arsenal. As Leo XIII wrote in *Aeternae Patris*, philosophy can be fought only by philosophy. Yet Rist finds the effort futile because to engage the contemporary mind, he believes, is to accept a terminology and terms of a debate foreign to one's own—a self-defeating exercise. He speaks of a Catch-22 situation. If the realist agrees to argue philosophically only in the restricted sense of the term as defined by the secularist, he will be starting anew with the tools and problems of secular philosophy. In doing so he may hone his own analytical skills, but it will be at the expense of ignoring his own and his opponent's foundations. It thus becomes easy to suppose that one has reached substantial agreement and common ground despite unresolvable disagreement over foundations. To argue with John Rawls, for example, is to fall into the trap of accepting his supposedly noncontroversial starting points, which, once accepted, lead by coherent logical steps to a hypothetical ethical construct, built actually on unsupported foundational principles. The realist in arguing with Rawls or his disciples must insist that his opponent can no more assume an inalienable value for the human being than they can the nonexistence of God. To demonstrate the harmony of a conceptual schema is not to demonstrate that such a system exists outside our own mind. Rist levels some sharp criticism at Catholic philosophers such as Germain Grisez, John Finnis, and John Haldane, who he thinks are vulnerable to accepting secular terms of debate at the expense of undermining the clarity of their own realist tradition.

Jacques Maritain, writing a dozen years after Santayana published the assessment quoted above, ended his Walgreen Lectures delivered at the University of Chicago with the judgment, "Sooner or later na-

18. Ibid.

tions will have to declare for or against the Gospel."[19] Maritain lectured from a manifestly Christian point of view. At issue was the nature of the public philosophy or belief system that supports the rule of law, one that is conducive to virtue in the citizens and their public institutions. Maritain saw clearly the difference between Christian and secular outlooks and their practical consequences. As sadly we have learned, requisite moral virtue in the citizenry has not been sustained by the secular humanism that has all but replaced Christianity as the public philosophy. Social theorists working from a purely secular point of view have begun to acknowledge such and have recognized the difficulty in reaching agreement with respect to "the good."

You may say that Rist has spent too much time at Oxford and Cambridge, that he ought to get out into the midlands and plains. Unfortunately, given the ubiquity of television and major print media, the countryside is no longer a refuge in which to escape secondhand smoke. Few—certainly no one in possession of a Catholic perspective—would deny that there has been in the past half-century a major cultural shift, with disastrous consequences for the individual as well as for the larger social order. The faith that unified Europe and its North American colonies has long been emasculated even in those academic centers to which it gave birth. Santayana was right: the shell of Christendom has been broken; the atheistic, socialist future is upon us.

Yet, paradoxically, we may be back at the beginning. The Church today resembles the Church of its early centuries, one in possession of truths about God, nature, and human nature, truths sorely needed by a pagan society. The problem is not simply one of communication. The first task is to understand what we have been given. The early Church Fathers, drawing upon all intellectual resources available in their efforts to understand and develop the faith, remain a model. We have the fruit of their efforts and two thousand years of reflection and commentary. "The wisdom of the Church" is not an idle phrase.

---

19. Jacques Maritain, *Man and the State* (Chicago: University of Chicago Press, 1951), 159.

To unlock that wisdom and recover its sources, the Church needs intellectual centers of the first order. Leo XIII saw the need and endorsed the founding of institutes of superior learning in France, Belgium, and the United States. We cannot claim that all of those institutes—call them universities—have remained true to their founding purpose. The Institute for the Psychological Sciences has been created out of the need to remedy the lapse. I was heartened to hear that the Legionaries of Christ not only are the sponsors of the institute but have established the University of Sacramento, California.

The first task confronting the Catholic intellectual milieu is to recover its own intellectual heritage. There is such a thing as a Catholic mind, a Protestant mind, and a purely secular mind, and there will always be such. Unfortunately, differences are not always acknowledged. One cannot consistently be a Catholic and a socialist. Either Christ is present in the Eucharist or He is not. Santayana himself inconsistently remained a cultural Catholic in spite of his loss of faith. He loved to meditate while seated at St. John Lateran, the pope's own church in Rome, choosing to end his life in the Eternal City. Differences between the Protestant, Catholic, and socialist mind are real and cannot be glossed over in the interest of a spurious harmony or in the name of ecumenism. Maritain puts it this way:

> The great utopian ideal of unity of all Christians can only be achieved with a complete disregard for the truth. One hears of "ecumenical dialogue" but not "ecumenical friendship." Is it not friendship which is first required—well-established habits of friendship, created by fraternal banquets, eating, drinking, and smoking together, conversing at random, and joking? Cheerful Christianity! Such is far more useful than the meetings of commissions with their endless programs, their interminable reports, and their stultifying speeches. The meal taken in common is the natural rite of human friendship.[20]

20. Jacques Maritain, *L'Eglise du Christ,* trans. J. W. Evans, *On the Church of Christ: The Person of the Church and Her Personnel* (Notre Dame, Ind.: University of Notre Dame Press, 1973), 111.

One of the first principles one learns in metaphysics is the principle of identity, which can be variously formulated as "A thing is what it is and no other," or "A thing must preserve its identity to preserve itself in being." For the Catholic mind, the first obligation is to know *what one holds.* Although that may require uncommon effort and a lifetime of study, we can learn from the accomplishment of others, as the early Church Fathers well understood. A mark of the Scholasticism that Luther despised is the conviction that philosophy, and *per extensionis* theology, is a science with conclusions that can be passed from one generation to another just as the Church has done so well through the centuries.

Early this month I was the guest of the Pontifical Academy of Science, incidentally an academy founded by Galileo, living testimony that the Church has long recognized the importance of higher learning. Today the Church lacks the resources of the modern state-supported university, which has all but excluded the type of learning characteristic of the great medieval universities and represented in the early decades of the last century by Désiré Mercier at Louvain and Edward A. Pace at the Catholic University of America. Christopher Dawson has often reminded us that the secular leviathan is vulnerable only at its brain. His dictum may be taken as a call not only to master our own tradition but to engage the secular mind. And here we have the advantage of two thousand years of intellectual history, two thousand four hundred if you include those grandfathers of the Church, Plato and "wretched Aristotle."

four

⊷

Robert Sokolowski

THE CHRISTIAN DIFFERENCE IN

PERSONAL RELATIONSHIPS

We wish to discuss the difference that Christian faith makes in the relationships that occur among persons. In order to develop this issue, we first should explore the understanding we have of persons. There are, of course, persons in God—the three persons of the Holy Trinity—and angels are persons too, but we wish to discuss the human person. In exploring this topic, I will especially draw on the work of Robert Spaemann, a German Catholic philosopher who is now emeritus professor at the University of Munich. I cannot recommend his writings too highly. I would especially like to use his book *Personen,* which has the marvelous subtitle *Versüche über den Unterschied zwischen "etwas" und "jemand"*[1]—Essays on the Distinction between "Something"

1. Robert Spaemann, *Personen: Versüche über den Unterschied zwischen "etwas" und "jemand"* (Stuttgart: Klett-Cotta, 1996).

and "Someone." The first point I wish to examine deals with an unusual feature that belongs to the "logic" of the word "person."

The Logic of Personal Terms

The strategic distinction that we need to make in order to bring out what we mean by the human person is the distinction between a human being and a human person. Every human being is a human person, but the meaning of each of these terms—the terms "human being" and "person"—is different, and if we can tease out this difference we will have made an important step in determining what the person is. Here is the way that Spaemann works out this difference.[2] He observes that the term "human being" or "man" is the name of a species or a genus of living things. These names are what philosophers of language call "sortal" terms, words that mark off a kind of entity, just as the terms "elephant" or "oak tree" or "spider" do. Such terms pick out or "sort out" one of the many species of things in the world: besides elephants, oak trees, spiders, and hydrogen atoms, there also are men or human beings. Such words name a universal. This universal, in turn, can have individuals that fall under it. We can speak about the genus *man* and we can also speak about individual men or human beings, just as we can use the word "tiger" to speak about both the species tiger as well as this or that tiger.

Now, we might be surprised to hear this, but the word "person" is not such a sortal term. It does not name a genus or species or kind of entity. It does not name a universal that encompasses a multitude of individuals. Rather, the term "person" is radically individualistic from the start. The term "person" is, in this respect, like the demonstrative pronoun "this." The term "this" cannot be used to mark off a genus or species; it too is not a sortal term. The term "this" is individualized every time we use it. It is formal and does not have a delimited content that is marked off from other kinds of things.

Spaemann illustrates this difference between sortal and nonsortal

2. Ibid., 14–19, 25.

terms in the following way. In regard to sortal terms, it makes sense for me to say to you, "Come here, I want to show you an oak tree," or "Come here, I want to show you a man (or a human being)." In such cases, I would be trying to show you an individual in a species. But it does not make sense for me to say to you, "Come here, I want to show you a person," no more than it would make sense for me to say, "Come here, I want to show you a this." Neither a person nor a this is an individual within a species. The logic of the term "person" is very tricky, much more puzzling than it might appear at first sight.

One might ask, "Why get into these logical conundrums? We want to hear about the person, about his dignity and originality and rights. Why should we care about sortal and nonsortal terms?" In reply to this objection, I would note that the logical peculiarity of the term "person" brings out the fact that each and every person is radically individualized. To express this feature of persons, I would like to introduce the term "singularity." Each person is a singularity. Each human person is not just a member of the species *homo sapiens,* but a singularity as well. Furthermore, each human being is more than an individual; Fido the dog and Leo the lion are individuals in their respective species, but they are not singularities, they are not persons. A human being, John or Jane, is both an individual in a species and also a singularity or a person. A human being is more radically individualized than is a dog or a lion. This difference is very important in dealing with things such as evolution or the physiological basis for human existence, or even for things such as cloning and issues related to the right to life. I would also claim that the Catholic belief that each human soul is individually created by God is related to the singularity of the human person.[3] Also, in things such as psychological counseling, it is important to realize that the therapist is dealing not just with an entity that needs to be made organically whole but also with a person who has a certain status and dignity as such. Finally, in the Middle Ages many thinkers

---

3. The singularity of persons is also reflected in the traditional belief that each angel is a species unto itself. One might just as well have said that each angel is a singularity. Angels do not share a nature in common; they are not individuals in a species.

who spoke about personhood stressed the incommunicability of the person, and my use of "singularity" is just a contemporary, phenomenological way of naming the same distinction.

So we have the human being and we have the person; the philosophical problem now is this: how do we reconcile these two things? How do we reconcile the fact that a human being is a member of a species, the species *man*, and also a singular person? The danger that lurks in this question is that we may say that there are two things in us: there is the human being and there is also the person, as two entities, with one somehow dwelling in the other. This would be a false and harmful approach. Somehow we have to show that there is only one thing, one entity, which is both an individualized nature and also a person. Animals and plants do not present this dilemma; they just are individuals in their species. They are subordinate to their species; even in the practical order, their existence is governed and exhausted by the well-being of the species. Human beings are also governed to some degree by their species and the inclinations that are natural to it, but in addition they exercise a government over themselves, and they do so because they are persons as well as individuals. They are not reducible to their species or their inclinations.

However, we must be careful not to go to the other extreme; we must not push this self-government into an existentialist excess; a Sartrean kind of self-creation would detach the person from the human being and make the person capable not only of governing his human nature but of creating it as he sees fit. Both extremes, the reductionist and the existentialist, must be avoided. Human beings both have a human nature and also govern themselves, but they must govern themselves in accordance with the truth of their human nature. How can both these dimensions be harmoniously thought together? We need to work out a distinction between the human being and the person, but we must avoid a separation between them.[4]

4. On the centrality of distinctions in philosophical thinking, see Robert Sokolowski, "Making Distinctions," *Review of Metaphysics* 32 (1979): 639–76, and "The Method of Philosophy: Making Distinctions," *Review of Metaphysics* 51 (1998): 515–32.

Reason as That Which Makes Us Persons

Why do human beings have this complexity, this duality of being both men and persons? It is our reason that makes the difference. One of the powers of human nature is reason or intelligence, and this power, which stems from our human being, makes us transcend our human being; it makes us to be persons and not just individuals. Our reason singularizes us and makes us subjects as well as members of a species. Because of our reason we share in the form of personal being that is proper to angels and even to God.

To refine our terminology, let us draw the distinction between soul and spirit. Soul is the animation of a body; every living thing has a soul: animals and plants are organic, animated beings, and so are men.[5] But besides having souls, human beings also have spirit, which involves the power of reason. Many thinkers, of course, have understood human beings as radically divided into two parts, the body and the spirit, and some have even thought that the rational part of the soul preexisted its life in the body. But in the Christian understanding, the spirit is the culminating part of the soul, and man is one being, not two. Man is both a human being and a person, and to formulate how these two dimensions come together is one of the perennial challenges for Christian thinking.

I would like to develop two ways in which human reason is manifested. These two themes will bring out more fully how reason establishes the singularity of persons. One way deals with cognition and the other with action.

First, the cognitional approach. When we thoughtfully articulate an object or a situation, we express it in speech; we make judgments. We say things like "The weather is improving," or "He has shown him-

5. On the difference between soul and spirit, see Robert Sokolowski, "Soul and the Transcendence of the Human Person," in *What Is Man, O Lord? The Human Person in a Biotech Age,* Proceedings of the Eighteenth Workshop for Bishops, ed. Edward A. Furton and Louise A. Mitchell (Boston: National Catholic Bioethics Center, 2002), 49–63.

self to be a liar," or "No one can take this from me." We exercise our reason when we articulate such things. Even if we are dealing with human emotions, there is an element of judgment and of reason in what we experience and express. If I am angry at you, it is because I think that you deserve this anger, that you have done something insulting or unjust to me or one of my own. Human emotion involves an opinion and hence it involves reason. The basic use of reason is to articulate a state of affairs and to express it in a judgment or statement or opinion. But then we can go one step further beyond this rational articulation; we can say things like "*I know* that the weather is improving," or "*I think* he is a liar," or "*I am* very angry with you." In expressions such as these, the use of the first-person pronoun, the use of the word "I," is special; I would like to call it the declarative use of the first person, as opposed to the merely informational use. What we do in such declarative usage is to confirm or ratify a certain statement or opinion. We explicitly appropriate the judgment we have made, and we mention ourselves as the ones who take responsibility for what we are saying. We do more than make an assertion; we put ourselves manifestly on the spot, we engage our responsibility in an explicit way, we declare ourselves. In our doing so, our personhood comes to the fore. Our singularity as cognitive agents is mentioned. I think that the declarative use of the first-person singular is a distinct and important phenomenological presentation of the human person.

Second, the domain of action. Here, our rationality and personhood come to the fore in the fact that we gradually become responsible, and are held to be responsible, for what we have become in our lives. We are not responsible for having been born as human beings, with all the emotions and inclinations that belong to our nature, but we do gradually make our own choices and appropriate our actions and thereby determine how we will be as human beings. Our choices do not only change things in the world; they also change us into being the way our choices are. We gradually specify the manner in which we will be inclined to act in the future. We are not responsible for being the kind of entity that can become angry, but we are in part responsible for the way in which our anger tends to be exercised. We are responsible, in large part, for our second nature, our character, for the shape that our natural inclinations and emotions have taken on.[6] We do not praise or blame an animal for being ferocious or submissive, but we do praise or blame human beings for becoming courageous, cowardly, or rash, for having become dissolute or frugal, prudent or frivolous. We may have been born with inclinations that tend toward one or other of these conditions, but in the end we have made the many choices that fixed our character along one line or another.

With these two points behind us, I think we can now say something a bit more precise about how our rational powers fit in with our human nature, how our personhood and our human being are related to one another. Once again, I wish to make use of Spaemann's thought.

Through our reason, we shepherd or cultivate our own concrete human being. Our human being, our concrete human nature, the nature we are born with, *will* develop in one way or another. It is something that is not complete when we are born; it will unfold, and how it unfolds depends on us. The ultimate responsibility for how this human being develops lies right within that human nature itself, in its rational power. We as persons cultivate *how* we exist as human beings. Animals and plants develop according to their nature and in response to circumstances, but they do not govern themselves, nor are they applauded or condemned for what they have done with their lives. There may be a statue for Man o' War in Lexington, Kentucky, but not, strictly speaking, because of what that horse did with his life; still less, incidentally, would we find a statue being put up for him by other horses. Animals and plants do not *lead* their lives, but we do lead our lives. The statue of Man o' War is different from a statue of Robert E. Lee or Stonewall Jackson. To put it in another way, as human beings we *have* our nature; we are not simply identical with it.

6. See Aristotle, *Nicomachean Ethics*, III 5.

We can take a certain distance to our concrete human being; as Spaemann puts it, "[Man] *has* a nature. Nature does not have him."[7] As persons we shepherd ourselves, and we must cultivate ourselves in accordance with the nature that we have.

These remarks will suffice, at present, for our discussion of the concept of person. Now we must turn to another theme, to the fact that we cannot cultivate ourselves in solitude. We cannot actualize our own human being without the presence and assistance of other human beings, that is, without being engaged in personal relationships.

Intersubjectivity

A human person cannot actualize and cultivate his human nature without the involvement of other people, other persons. It is not the case that our cognition or our action can take place within us simply as individuals. Our cognition and our actions are not merely natural processes.

Consider, for example, the judgments that we make. Judgments or opinions do not arise in us simply as a result of an internal natural process. It is not the case that a judgment occurs when a sensory impact is elevated into intellectual cognition by some sort of activity in the brain or by the intervention of cognitive faculties such as the agent intellect. A judgment is not a solitary thing that just takes place within us, no more than a vote or a complaint is a solitary thing. *We* as cognitive agents have to achieve our judgments, and we do so in relation with others. What happens when we engage in a judgment is that one person draws the attention of another person toward some object, and then says something about that object. In its original form, a judgment occurs between people. Only subsequently, and only after we become quite sophisticated, do we become capable of making judgments for ourselves alone, of thinking simply in solitude. Our

7. Spaemann, *Personen,* 105.

cognitive abilities become actualized among people, and they also depend on a lot of emotional forces: we have to have a sense of security, of self-confidence, of patience in order to refer to things and to truthfully say something about them. Even the imposition of names on things takes place among people; for a child to learn that a certain sound is the name of some object, the child must realize that someone else is using that name to refer to that thing.[8] If an object and a sound merely come together, the child may associate the sound with the object but will not take the sound to be the name of the thing. The person becomes activated as an agent of truth in reciprocity with other people. The mind or the reason of the person becomes activated intersubjectively.

It should be even more obvious that human moral action also develops only in interaction with others. The virtues of justice and friendship obviously could occur only when we act with and toward other people, but even the more subjective virtues of temperance and courage can be developed only under the guidance of others. Temperance and courage require a rational form, the structure of a middle between extremes; they are thoughtful virtues, not just impulses. Other people share their virtue and their moral assessments, their prudence, with us as they open up for us the possibility of living a life in accordance with virtue. It is true that some people may be able on their own to transcend a debased and hopeless moral environment, that their goodness may seem to come almost from nowhere or almost entirely from within them; I believe that such a person is what Aristotle calls the "godlike" man.[9] But even such people require other persons as foils to stimulate their own entrance into moral excellence.

8. See Paul Bloom, *How Children Learn the Meaning of Words* (Cambridge, Mass.: MIT Press, 2000), 55–87. See also the excellent book by Kyra Karmiloff and Annette Karmiloff-Smith, *Pathways to Language: From Fetus to Adolescent,* Developing Child Series (Cambridge, Mass.: Harvard University Press, 2001).

9. On the godlike, see Aristotle, *Nicomachean Ethics,* VII 1, and also the important cryptic remark in X 9, 1179b22–23.

I would like to add one more point in regard to the intersubjective character of moral action. It deals with the role of friendship in human conduct. Traditionally, friendship is not listed among the moral virtues. The classical "cardinal virtues" are courage, temperance, prudence, and justice. However, I have tried to argue that in Aristotle's *Nicomachean Ethics* friendship plays a much more central role in the discussion of the moral virtues. Several virtues, including courage and temperance, are treated in books III and IV, and justice is discussed in book V, but friendship is treated in two books, books VIII and IX, toward the end of the work. I think that friendship, and specifically noble friendship, is the culmination of moral virtue; the ability to be a friend in the highest and best way is the moral perfection of human nature, according to Aristotle. Justice is not the highest virtue after all; friendship is. Friendship is beyond justice. In perfect and noble friendship, the friends wish well toward each other specifically in their respective individualities, and their friendship makes it possible for them to accomplish things they never could have done apart from the friendship. I would also like to claim that all the other virtues, even those of courage and temperance, participate in friendship; in courage and temperance we become friends with ourselves, as we attain harmony between our reason on the one hand and our desires and aversions on the other. It should also be clear, I think, that justice can be seen as a participation in friendship.[10]

If friendship does have this exalted role in human moral excellence, then it is all the more clear that we become virtuous only through our activity with other people and toward other people, just as we actualize our reason only with other people and toward other people. Our personhood is actualized intersubjectively, even in the natural order. Such perfection occurs first in familial relationships, of course, as the child learns to speak and interact in response to his

---

10. On the place of the virtue of friendship in moral philosophy, see Robert Sokolowski, "Friendship and Moral Action in Aristotle," *Journal of Value Inquiry* 35 (2001): 355–69, and "Phenomenology of Friendship," *Review of Metaphysics* 55 (2002): 451–70.

mother's initiatives and reactions, but such a familial achievement could not be the highest form of human personal existence. As important and as fundamental as it may be, it would become stifling if it were made into the largest context. The human person has to expand beyond the family into the village and then into the city, or at least into whatever approximation to the city he is fortunate or unfortunate enough to live in. Political life, with its virtues of justice and civic friendship, perfects the human being, and it even brings prepolitical societies to their own excellence. A family that is deprived of a political context is less excellent as a family. The intersubjectivity that allows human beings to be actualized as persons extends as far as the political domain.

There is a passage in Henry James's *The Ambassadors* that brings out the difference between the human being and the person and that also shows the connection between personhood and human relations. At one point in the story, Lambert Strether looks back on his life and the many disappointments in it: "the fact that he had failed, as he considered, in everything, in each relation and in half a dozen trades."[11] The narrator in the novel then says, about Strether's life: "Though there had been people enough all round it there had been but three or four persons *in* it."[12] James distinguishes between *people* and *persons*. Only a handful of other human beings were fully engaged in Strether's life, as rational and moral agents, hence as persons. All the others simply "stood around" his life; they were there just as individuals, as human beings taken in a generic but uninvolved sense.

The Christian Dimension

In the rest of my paper, I will discuss how Christian faith and Christian understanding modifies the personal relations we have been examining. It was necessary for me to spend a lot of time on the

11. Henry James, *The Ambassadors* (New York: W. W. Norton, 1964), 61.
12. Ibid.

person and on intersubjectivity in order to provide the context within which the Christian difference comes into play.

In our spontaneous, natural understanding, the understanding that we find expressed, for example, in Plato and Aristotle or in pagan religious writers, we take the world as the ultimate whole of things, the ultimate context. The divine principle is the highest, best, and most powerful element in this whole, in this world or cosmos. The divine is the governing and sacred element. But Christianity radically adjusts this understanding. It takes the whole of things, the cosmos or the sum of all entities, not as the unquestionable background against which all things, including the divine, are determined; rather, it takes the whole of things as being there because of a creative choice on the part of God. This God, this divinity, is then understood as not having needed to create, as being so perfect and subsistent that no perfection could be added to him. The world is seen as created out of a freedom and generosity that satisfies no need on the part of the Creator.

Christian faith, obedient to divine revelation in the Old and New Covenants, also believes that this God, who created the world out of sheer generosity, became part of the world in the Incarnation; in the person of the Word, the divine nature became joined with a human nature. The Incarnation also reveals to us the inner life of God, the truth that God is not a solitary being but a Trinity of Persons even while remaining one God. What do these articles of Christian faith—Creation, Incarnation, and the Holy Trinity—imply for the human person and for interpersonal relationships? I would like to discuss two major topics.

The first topic is the difference that occurs in regard to human moral conduct. We have seen that it is possible to consider friendship as the highest virtuous activity in the moral domain. However, for pagan thinking, the highest friendships we are capable of are, quite naturally, those that occur among human beings. According to Aristotle, friendship with god or the gods is impossible, because the difference between mortal and immortal beings is too great: "When one party is removed to a great distance, as god is, the possibility of friendship ceases."[13] But in Christian faith, we believe that God became man and invited us to friendship with him. In chapter 15 of St. John's Gospel, during the discourse at the Last Supper, Jesus says to his disciples, "You are my friends if you do what I command you." He calls them friends, *philoi,* and he goes on to draw a contrast: "I no longer call you slaves, because a slave does not know what his master is doing." A slave does what the master commands, but he does so blindly; he does not understand the thinking of the master. Christ does not want that kind of obedience from those who follow him; rather, he continues, "I have called you friends, because I have told you everything I have heard from my Father." The reason the disciples are his friends is that they have been introduced into the truth of the relationship between Christ and the Father; they now are capable of understanding in faith, and so they are friends and not slaves.

We should not underestimate the startling originality of such statements. To say that human beings can be friends of God, and that they have received the truth of God's own life, is truly overwhelming. The idea that we could be friends with the first principle of the universe is something that would sound like utter foolishness to pagan thinkers; they would see it as totally lacking in sobriety and realism. This friendship with God is made possible by the incarnate presence of the Son of God; we can become friends of Christ and hence share in his Sonship. Furthermore, the focus of this new truth and this new status is on God himself. What this new truth reveals is not so much how wonderful *we* are—we did not and could not have earned this friendship by anything we might have done—but how all-powerful God is; God could humiliate himself in the Incarnation and in Christ's atoning death, and still remain the eternally omnipotent and glorious Creator of everything that is. No human being could have imagined a God like this. We know of this God, this divinity, only because Christ has

13. Aristotle, *Nicomachean Ethics,* VIII 7, 1158b1159a4–5.

told us everything he heard from the Father, and we must respond by doing what he has commanded us. Without Christ we would not have dared to think such things. We have to be called to faith and must respond in obedience.

Furthermore, because Christ draws us into this form of friendship with God, it becomes possible for us to declare ourselves, to use the first-person singular pronoun in our relationship to God himself. We can say "I believe," or "I love," or "I beseech," not only before other people but also before and toward God. Through the words of Christ we know that God hears us; we come to know that such declarations are not just imaginary exercises or empty self-deceptions. We speak and declare ourselves not only before other men but also before God; we therefore act as agents of truth before God; we exercise our rational cognition and our rational action, which now are elevated by grace into a set of exchanges that would not be possible or conceivable as part of our natural endowment. This life with God, in which we act as friends of Christ and adopted sons of the Father, is based on truth, not on blind obedience, and hence it elevates our rational personhood, our agency in truth. I think that this theme of the enhancement of truth that faith brings has been developed in a moving way by the writings of Pope John Paul II, especially in his encyclicals *Veritatis Splendor* and *Fides et Ratio*.

I should also like to mention that this new friendship with God, in grace and in charity, is anticipated in the Old Covenant. Consider the psalms, where the psalmist, and the believer who prays the psalms, repeatedly addresses God and glorifies and thanks him, expresses sorrow for sins, and petitions him for his help. In the psalms as well as in the prayers of Abraham, Moses, and the prophets, human beings begin to declare themselves before Jahweh. God's radical transcendence is not compromised by this intervention in the world, through which he chooses a people and guides them in providence, and in which he allows them to address him. But this providential presence of God in the world reaches a greater intensity when God not only intervenes in the world but also becomes part of it and allows us to address him in friendship in his incarnate presence. Through grace we become able to act as agents of truth before the Father.

The second major topic I wish to examine is the interpersonal relationships that exist within the Most Holy Trinity. Here I wish to discuss how the divine nature is related to the three persons of the Trinity. When we spoke about the human person, we tried to show how the person is distinguished from the human being, from the man, from the concrete instance of human nature. We showed that the concrete human nature needs to be developed, to be shepherded throughout its life. We are not born in a perfect condition; as human beings our lives and inclinations need to be brought to a finished state by the choices we make. As we lead our lives, it is our rationality, both theoretic and practical, that enables us to cultivate our nature and bring it to its state of happiness or frustration. We have dominion over our acts and we lead our lives. In this human condition, each of us is one human being and one person: we have one life and one governing power within that life. Human rationality is distributed among individual substances and singular persons.

In God, however, there is one divine nature but three persons, Father, Son, and Holy Spirit. And obviously the divine nature is not something that needs to be cultivated and brought to completion; it is not like our natures, which are born imperfect. The divine nature is eternally the perfection of existence. How are the persons in the Holy Trinity related to this divine nature? They do not strive to perfect it, but they are distinguished by the way in which they bestow and receive it. The Father is distinguished from the Son through the action of generation.[14] In this action, the Father expresses himself totally in the Word that is generated; as Jesus says in St. John's Gospel, "Everything that the Father has is mine" (Jn 16:15). In the same Gospel, Jesus addresses the Father and says, "Everything of mine is yours and everything of yours is mine" (Jn 17:10). Christ does not say these

14. *Summa theologiae* (*ST*) Ia, q. 28, a. 4.

things only as a man; he also expresses his divine life and being as having been given to him by the Father. The divine nature, everything that the Father is or has, is given over to the Son, who receives it from the Father. The Holy Spirit, the third person of the Trinity, is distinguished by the action of spiration, in which the Spirit proceeds from the Father and the Son together. These actions and receptions—generation and filiation, spiration and procession, as St. Thomas Aquinas names them[15]—are all internal to the Holy Trinity, and they permit there to be a community in the one true God. As Aquinas says, "If there were not a plurality of persons in the divinity, it would follow that God would be alone or solitary."[16]

These three persons are distinguished by the way the divine nature is given and received. It might be misleading to say that the Father *gives* the divine nature to the Son, because that would seem to imply that this donation was a matter of choice, the way creation is. Within the Holy Trinity, the Father essentially expresses himself in his internal Word; this expression is called a generation, and so the Word is also the Son. As St. Thomas says, "The Father does not generate the Son by an act of will [*voluntate*], but by nature."[17] According to St. Thomas, the generation of the Son is done by way of intelligence, and the generation of the Holy Spirit is done by way of the will. The two spiritual powers in the divine nature, intelligence and will, issue in the Son and the Holy Spirit. In the appropriate sense of giving, however, we could say that the Father gives the divine nature to the Son, who receives it from him, and the Father and the Son give the divine nature to the Holy Spirit, who receives it from them. As St. Thomas says, "The Holy Spirit . . . accepts the nature of the Father, just as the Son does."[18]

We could not say, therefore, that the divine persons perfect the divine nature, but it could be said that they give and receive it. It is in

---

15. Ibid.

16. Ibid., q. 31, a. 3, ad 1.

17. Ibid., q. 42, a. 2. See also q. 41, a. 2.

18. Ibid., q. 35, a 2.

the nature of God that he gives and receives, so charity or generosity makes up the life of the Holy Trinity. As St. John says in his first letter, "God is love" (1 Jn 4:8, 4:16). The Father does not just give some of what he is, or some of what he has; he gives everything, the entire divine nature, to the Son. This total giving within the Trinity is reflected in the death of Jesus, in which, through the dominion he had over his actions, he handed over his incarnate life and being, his entire human nature, for our salvation. The crucifixion is therefore an icon of the charity within the interpersonal life of God, and the Resurrection bears witness that this charity and life are not overcome by either sin or death.

Through Christ's action and through grace, we are enabled to become friends of the incarnate Son of God. We also learn, if we are attentive to the words of Christ and the inspiration of the Holy Spirit, that the life within God is trinitarian and generous, a kind of friendship beyond human measure. It is only logical, then, that our own human relationships should reflect these truths. St. John's first letter tells us, "Let us love one another, because love is from God" (1 Jn 4:7). There would be something grotesque in accepting the truth about the divine nature and then acting in a way that contradicts it. As Christians, our actions and our lives are profiled against the background of the Holy Trinity and the Incarnation. The charity we are called to, however, does not override the demands of the natural human virtues, such as temperance and courage, justice and prudence, and also human friendship. These things have their own logic and their own necessity, but they are now understood as participating in the goodness of the God who created them out of sheer generosity.

Christian revelation, therefore, confirms human personal relationships even as it takes us beyond them. It does so because it confirms human reason, the reason that makes us persons, even as it raises us beyond reason into belief in the Word of God.

five

Richard John Neuhaus

NEWMAN'S SECOND SPRING—

ONCE AGAIN

Two years after the reestablishment of the hierarchy in England, the theme of a second spring preoccupied John Henry Cardinal Newman. In July of 1852 he was asked to address the bishops, and said the following:

> The world grows old, but the Church is ever young. Arise, Mary, and go forth in thy strength, into that North Country which once was thine own. A second temple rises on the ruins of the old. Canterbury has gone its way. York is gone. Durham is gone. Winchester is gone, but the Church in England has died and the Church lives again. Westminster and Nottingham, Beverly and Exemen, North Hampton and Shrewsbury, if the world lasts, shall be names as musical to the ear, as stirring to the heart as the glories we have lost. And saints shall

rise out of them, if God so will, and doctors of the Church once again shall give the law to Israel and preachers call to penance and to justice as at the beginning.[1]

Pope John Paul II spoke repeatedly—some would say incessantly, some might even say obsessively—about springtime, a springtime of evangelization; he spoke about the beginning of the third millennium as a springtime of Christian unity, a springtime for the Church to be born again in its mission to enable the birth again of a tired world.

It is twenty years since I published a book called *The Catholic Moment,*[2] with which some of you might be familiar, and in which I contended that the premier responsibility for the Christian mission rests with the Catholic Church—so it seemed to me then as a Lutheran pastor—the premier opportunity and therefore, responsibility for evangelization, for cultural transformation in America and the world. When I am asked whether the Catholic moment has passed, the answer is that if the Catholic Church is what she proposes herself to be, and I have no doubt that she is that, then all moments between Pentecost and our Lord's return in glory are the Catholic moment.

My friend Peter Steinfels, some five years after the book was published, wrote a column in the *New York Times—Week in Review,* in which the heading was "Has the Catholic Moment Passed?" And in his fine journalistic way he surveyed various news on this question and finally ended up more or less saying: yes, it's past. I talked to Peter afterward and I said, "You know this is a column not without metaphysical, philosophical interest because when the book came out, you said there was no Catholic moment and now five years later it's been here and gone. This is interesting."

1. *Sermons Preached on Various Occasions* (New York: Longmans and Green, 1908). John Henry Cardinal Newman preached this sermon on July 13, 1852, in St. Mary's College, Oscott, in the First Provincial Synod of Westminster, before Cardinal Wiseman and the bishops of England.

2. *The Catholic Moment: The Paradox of the Church in the Postmodern World* (New York: HarperCollins, 1987).

What I'd like to focus on is all these signs of springtime that John Paul II discerned and called us to discern and to respond to. I'd like to speak about the future of the family and the Church's witness and what needs to be done and has been done. In *Familiaris Consortio* *(FC)*, the 1981 apostolic exhortation on the family in the modern world, there is this marvelous phrase, "Humanity's passage to the future is through the family" *(FC,* n. 86). The argument is that to care about the human project is to care about the family, and the Church cares lovingly, intensively, passionately about the human project. The family today, needless to say, is challenged on many, many different fronts and in many different ways, but it all begins with and it ever comes back to the question of faith and the challenges to the family. Catholic teaching on questions of the family and human relationships are modeled in a familial form toward a telos, toward an end of community that is not untouched by intimations of and grace from the community of God Himself: Father, Son, and Holy Spirit.

The Church has a doctrine of the faith, a truth divinely inspired and humanly informed regarding marriage and the family. And with this truth she challenges the Catholic faithful and the world. Families that respond to the challenge of faith are equipped to meet the many other challenges that will surely come their way. This we must say again and again, that with faith everything is possible and without it all foundations rest upon shifting sand. In reflecting on family life and so much else, we are haunted by the question of our Lord, when the Son of Man returns, will he find faith on earth? (Lk 18:8) Now it is no secret that the Church's teaching on sexuality and marriage and family is ignored by many Catholics and is derided by perhaps most outside the Church. This is not to say that the teaching is rejected, for to be rejected it must be, at least at some modest level, understood, and to be understood it must be taught, and as most of us are aware, too frequently the Church's truth about marriage and the family is not taught. It is not taught confidently; it is not taught persistently; it is not taught winsomely; it is not taught with conviction.

It is not taught in part because in our culture it is frequently derided and distorted. The media are, it is cliché to observe by now, captive to a very distorted and distortive version of the Catholic story. And a central component of that story, accented again and again and again with boring predictability, is the claim that most Catholics dissent from the Church's teaching on sexuality and family life. But of course that claim is highly doubtful, for again, to dissent one must know what it is that one is dissenting from. And yet that claim, reiterated again and again, repeated often enough, has an intimidating and an inhibiting effect upon the Catholic people and upon catechists and upon priests, and we may even suggest perhaps upon some bishops. Repeated often enough—and it is repeated incessantly—it insinuates the suspicion that in this vital area of human life the effective teaching of Catholic doctrine is a losing cause, perhaps an already lost cause.

Again, I think our situation is accurately described in terms not of dissent but of widespread ignorance and confusion. Admittedly, the problem is compounded by the fact that there are some, all too many, who do dissent: theologians and others who are not above employing ignorance and confusion in an effort to advance their own views. One speaks of this with sorrow and hesitation, and yet, speak of it we must. It is not a matter of making allegations, for those responsible could hardly be more public in identifying their views and declaring their purposes. Theirs is not the quiet and conscientious dissent of scholarly service to the Church, aimed at helping the Church to articulate the truth ever more fully and persuasively. Rather it is a different kind of dissent altogether, a dissent of bitter opposition and angry alienation, a dissent that confuses opinion research with the *sensus fidelium,* and attributes magisterial authority to the signs of the times, as authoritatively expressed by academic guilds and the prestige media.

This is the phenomenon addressed, no doubt with a heavy heart, by the Holy Father on so many different occasions. In *Veritatis Splendor* (*VS,* n. 113), for example, that splendid encyclical, John Paul II says, "Dissent in the form of carefully orchestrated protests and polemics carried on in the media is opposed to ecclesial communion and to a correct understanding of the hierarchical constitution of the people of God." As this pope affirmed again and again, revealed moral doctrine is truly doctrine of the faith, and what is at stake is infinitely more than intramural squabbles between liberals and conservatives, progressives and traditionalists. What is at stake is whether people understand that they are invited to the high moral drama of Christian discipleship, of living in the truth. To put it very bluntly, souls are at stake. And if we do not believe that souls are at stake, we must seriously ask ourselves what business we think we are in.

After recent scandal and disarray and dissembling, it becomes even more difficult for the Church to issue in a believable, winsome, persuasive way the invitation to the high adventure of discipleship. But some things perhaps may be more hopeful. Please God, we have behind us those long years of celebrity dissent, of bitter acrimony, of tediously publicized irascibility. It is time to move on. It is past time to move on. The Church has not the time. The world has not the time. Countless men and women eager to live the adventure to holiness have not the time for interminable intramural disputes that obscure the splendor of Christian truth about marriage and family.

If we have the will for it, if we have the wit for it, if we have most importantly the faith for it, the world that has lost its way is waiting to receive the gift of the Church, which is the good news of the One who is the way. And a world that has come to doubt the very existence of truth waits to hear from the One who is the truth. And a world falling headlong into a culture of death looks with desperate hope to the One who said, "I am the way and the truth and the life" (Jn 14:6). If we have the will for it, and the wit for it, and the faith for it, this is our moment, and the Catholic moment, which is every moment, and is most certainly this moment in time.

At the beginning of the third millennium, we stand amidst the rubble of the collapsed delusions of a modernity that sought freedom in life by liberating itself from the author and the end of life. And many of the best and the brightest announced the death of God, but what appeared is now abundantly evident, the death of man. It is for man, for the human, for men and women in their personal dignity and vocation to holiness that the Church contends. In almost every major document in his pontificate, John Paul II tirelessly reiterated that the revelation of God in Christ, citing *Gaudium et Spes* 22, is not only the revelation of God to man, but the revelation of man to himself.

Avery Cardinal Dulles has aptly said that the teaching of John Paul II should be described as prophetic humanism. This is the prophetic humanism that the Church proposes to a world that is wearied and wasted by false humanisms that deny both man's nature and his transcendent glory. The Church neither can nor wants to impose this authentic humanism on the contemporary world. There is a marvelous expression in the encyclical *Redemptoris Missio (RM)*, the Mission of the Redeemer, in which the Holy Father takes up the question: Is it not something of an intrusion and a violation of pluralism and difference for the Church to propose that the gospel of Jesus Christ is for everyone? And then he responds, saying, "The Church imposes nothing. She only proposes" (*RM,* n. 39). The Church imposes nothing. She only proposes. But if we understand the crisis and the opportunity of our historical moment, we will propose the truth and do so urgently and winsomely and persuasively and persistently, as St. Paul says to Timothy, "in season and out of season" (2 Tm 4:2).

I am convinced that there is reason to hope that after the long winter of jaded discontent, the modern world may be entering a season of greater receptivity to the truth that the Church has to offer. The great British novelist Anthony Burgess sometimes described himself as an apostate Catholic, but shortly before he died, he wrote this: "My apostasy had never been perfect. I am still capable of moaning and breast-beating at my defection from, as I recognize it, the only system that makes spiritual and intellectual sense." Like the apostasy of Mr. Burgess, the apostasy of our world from Christian truth is by no means perfect.

John Paul II, again, spoke of a springtime of evangelization, of ecumenism, of faith. He could not know, and we cannot know, what is
in store for us in the remainder of this century, never mind whatever centuries more there will be before our Lord's return. We cannot
know, but we can be prepared. We can be prepared to be surprised by
a time in which thoughtful men and women will give a new hearing
to the only truth that, as Mr. Burgess says, "makes spiritual and intellectual sense."

With respect to the family or anything else, one runs a risk of
course by suggesting that the world needs to hear, whether it knows
it or not, the truth that the Church has to offer. One runs the risk of,
among other things, being accused of triumphalism. But if the alternative to triumphalism is defeatism, I'll take triumphalism any day, always remembering that the only triumph that we seek is the triumph
already secured by the One who came, as he said of himself, "not to
be served but to serve" (Mt 20:28). Springtime may not produce immediate results; it's in the nature of springtime. Indeed at times the
results may seem more like failure, but we know that "unless a grain
of wheat falls into the earth and dies, it remains alone, but if it dies,
it bears much fruit" (Jn 12:24). And there were seeds sown long ago
in cultures once called Christian, seeds that may again be breaking
through the earth that has for so long been hard frozen, under the ice
of indifference and unbelief. I take it that this is what the Holy Father
meant when he so earnestly called us to the tasks of re-evangelization,
to evangelize and to re-evangelize, to sow anew and to nurture to new
life what is already sown, but has for so long been stunted and stifled
by neglect and faithless distraction.

The Church is always and relentlessly the sower who went out to
sow, and some seeds fell on rocky ground and some among the thorns
and some fell on good ground and brought forth grain, a hundredfold
and sixty and thirty. And at the end of the parable, our Lord says, "He
who has ears to hear, let him hear." That of course is what we must
pray for, that we may hear and help others to hear, the splendor of

Christian truth regarding also marriage and the family. It is difficult to make the case.

We can easily get discouraged, but we have not the right to despair, and finally, we have not the reason to despair. The words of the psalmist we make our own: "He that goes forth weeping, bearing the seed shall come home rejoicing bringing in the sheaves." If in anticipating the springtime of the beginning of this millennium, we are to sow more confidently and more effectively, if our sowing is to transform the world—and we are called to do nothing less than that—we ourselves must be transformed. And it seems to me that there are number of transformations of pressing urgency within the life of the Church. Five come to mind, but the number is somewhat arbitrary. We need, first, to cultivate intelligently the courage to be countercultural; second, to appropriate more fully the gift of Peter among us, a gift luminously exemplified by John Paul II's pontificate; third, to recognize that the Church's teaching about sexuality and marriage and the family has a coherent structure, that it is all of a piece; fourth, more fully to honor marriage as a Christian vocation, and to demonstrate that we do so; and finally, to have an intensified commitment to what *Familiaris Consortio* calls "the politics of the family." Let me touch on these just briefly.

Whether "in season or out of season" (2 Tm 4:2), as St. Paul puts it, those who propose Christian truth must always cultivate the courage to be countercultural. Until our Lord returns in glory we will be wrestling with what it means to be in the world but not of the world, and never getting it quite right. The truth that the Church proposes is for the world, but the Church will inevitably appear to be against the world when the world resists the truth about itself. Again, section 22 of *Gaudium et Spes:* the necessary posture of prophetic humanism must therefore be one of being against the world for the world. Moreover, cultural resistance to the truth has many more formidable sources. With St. Paul, we never forget that "we are," in his words, "contending, not against flesh and blood, but against the principalities, against the powers, against the world rulers of this present darkness, against the spiritual hosts of wickedness in heavenly places" (Eph 6:12).

Especially in North America, many fear that the call to be countercultural, the call for countercultural courage, is an invitation to return to what is derisively called ghetto Catholicism of an earlier period. But that is not the case. Sociologically speaking, immigrant Catholicism in this country was not so much countercultural as subcultural. The progression is to move from subcultural striving to cultural achievement to countercultural challenge and transformation. The remarkable cultural success of American Catholics in the last half century is a tragic failure if it means, as some take it to mean, that now Catholics are just like everybody else. Real success is marked by the confidence and courage to challenge the culture of which we are securely part; or to put it differently, there is a crucial difference between being American Catholics and being Catholic Americans. The adjective is the controlling factor. We are constantly being told there is a distinctively American way of being Catholic, but the course of countercultural courage is to demonstrate that there is a distinctively Catholic way of being American. The Catholic moment happens when American Catholics discover and dare to act upon what it means to be Catholic Americans.

An earlier generation prided itself on being accepted by American culture, and we should honor what was honorable, so much that was honorable, in that achievement. But surely today the task is to prepare a generation that will dare not to strive for acceptance in American culture, but to transform American culture, to be Catholic Americans. Catholicism in the United States is no longer, as it so often did understand itself to be, a suppliant of sorts, standing hat in hand before its cultural betters. We are full participants who unhesitatingly accept our responsibility to remedy a culture that is descending in decadence and disarray. The remedy begins with each person who hears and responds to the radical call to holiness, in accord with moral truth, *Veritatis Splendor*. That is the message also of *Familiaris Con-*

sortio, where it reads, "In a particular way, the Church addresses the young, who are beginning their journey toward marriage and family life, for the purpose of presenting them with new horizons, helping them to discover the beauty and the grandeur of the vocation to love and the service of life" (*FC* n. 1). And that is also the message of *Veritatis Splendor,* that we are called to nothing less than moral greatness.

I met a friend of Karol Wojtyla's, in Krakow, an old man who knew him back when he was a teenager, and we were discussing what there was about Karol Wojtyla as Pope John Paul II that so powerfully, so electrically attracted the devotion and imagination of young people. And he said, Oh, Lolek," referring to the pope by his nickname as a young man. He said, "Oh, Lolek, I've been watching him all these years. And he just keeps saying the same thing. He just finds a thousand different ways to say it." And I said, "Well, so what is this thing that he's saying?" And he said, "When I was a young man, and when he was a young priest and when he was bishop here, and all the years he's been pope, he's just been saying, especially to young people: settle for nothing less than moral and spiritual greatness."

"Settle for nothing less than moral and spiritual greatness." And so it is that we must settle for nothing less and urge others to settle for nothing less and persuade the Catholic people to settle for nothing less. One time when I was with the Holy Father, he asked, as he always did, how John Cardinal O'Connor was doing, and I would always give him a good report, as you might imagine. I said, "You know what he said, Holy Father, the other day?" And he said, "No what did he say?" "He said he gets up every morning and prays that he'll go to bed that night without having discouraged any impulse of the Holy Spirit." I said, "Isn't that a beautiful thing for a bishop to say, Holy Father?" And the Holy Father says, "Yes, that is very beautiful. I told him that." But whoever came up with it first, it is of a piece with this settling for nothing less than greatness. We are told that young people today are immersed in a hedonistic culture of self-gratification, consumerism, and so on, deaf to the call of moral greatness. I simply don't believe that. I think what we saw in response to John Paul II, what all of us have seen in our own lives—the guard of the students who gather at Krakow; the Legionaries of Christ; the new group in New York, World Youth Alliance, most astonishing young people from all over the world who are just on fire, and joyfully on fire with zeal—is a joyful zeal, a healthy zeal, to live and to invite others to live the high adventure of Catholic fidelity.

While there are many changes that are needed if the Church is to exemplify the adventure to which she invites others, we need to more fully appropriate the gift of Peter among us, as represented in the astonishing years of John Paul II's pontificate. We have witnessed before our eyes the vibrant Spirit-guided development of the Church's heart and mind, the development that John Henry Cardinal Newman celebrated as "the distinctive and unique and finally decisively different charism of the Catholic Church." And yet it must be said that the gift of Peter among us, in this embodiment, has not been truly received by us. The teaching of John Paul II's pontificate, it seems to me, hardly began to penetrate the institutions and practices of American Catholicism. We witness the enormous resistance to *Ex Corde Ecclesiae,* a bold proposal for revitalizing the excitement of Catholic education. And how many timorous, fearful people view it simply as a regression, as a restoration of an authoritarian structure, as a denial of academic freedom? Instead of seeing that it is precisely a case of the Church proposing—imposing nothing—but proposing a way of fidelity. If the invitation is accepted, then in response to the great *Yes* of the invitation there will be other *No*s, which some people will view as an unhappy consequence. But every *No* is premised upon a greater *Yes*—that this gift of Peter among us, whether in higher education or whether in family policy or in a host of other areas, has not been fully received, not in the catechetical life of Catholicism in the United States.

That too may be changing. A younger generation is little interested in the tired ecclesiastical politics of the more than forty years since

the end of the council, and the same old wrangling, conservative versus liberal, progressive versus traditionalist, liberationist versus magisterial. The younger generation want to get on with it, with the brac-
ing adventure of being authentically Catholic. Those who have kept
alive for all these years the scratching of their discontents, the chronic
complaining, they now, in order to recruit, have to replicate the world
of real and imagined grievance by which their cause was created. And
they can't do that, just by chronological given. Anybody been born in
the last forty years cannot remember, has no experience of, cannot
even conjure the image of this putatively oppressive, ghettoized, pre–
Vatican II Catholic Church, against which the liberationist cause is
launched. It has certainly been my experience, not only with such as
the Legionaries of Christ, but in our seminaries around the country,
that there's an older generation that says that these priests now, these
young men entering the priesthood—entering the seminary, being ordained—are timorous and dull and conformist and rigidly orthodox
and so forth. And perhaps there are some who fit that description, no
doubt. But I find that there are many more who are eager to be enlist-
ed in the great cause, to throw their lives away for something of im-
measurably greater worth than any of us ever have a right to expect.
In a marvelous phrase, the archbishop of Milwaukee, Tim Dolan, who
has long experience in seminary education and was the rector also of
the North American College in Rome, says, "A young man will throw
his life away for a mystery, but not for a question mark." His point is
that over the last forty years, the priesthood was turned into a question mark for too many young men, too many parents, too many in
the Church.

To cultivate the courage to be countercultural, to appropriate the
gift of this pontificate, to recognize that the Church's teaching on sexuality and marriage and family is all of a piece, here it is unavoidable
at least to mention *Humanae Vitae*. Much of the theological energy of
a generation and more has been dissipated in rancorous dispute over
that encyclical, an encyclical greeted by a highly organized, orches-

trated campaign of dissent and indeed rejection. Surely it is time to move on, at least to understand what the Catholic proposal is, with respect to the nature of the conjugal act and the conjugal act within the whole invitation to holiness. There are a few academics who will continue to fret about whether this teaching of the church is infallible or irreformable. But the Catholic people cannot live well the lives to which they are called if they live with a sense of uncertainty, of contingency, of conditionality about the moral truth that claims their allegiance—if they are told that while this is the teaching today, maybe tomorrow or five years from now it'll be such and such. The proposal must be made; we owe it to the Catholic people. They have a right to have the proposal presented, which is not to say that it is a proposal easy to live.

It's not to say that there aren't innumerable pastoral problems with respect to the understanding that the Church proposes of marriage, and family, and sexuality. Of course there are all kinds of problems, but people must know that a certain proposal is on the table. Maybe without that people are led, as I say, to a Catholicism of conditionality, which is a Catholicism of confusion.

People are led to think that the Church will change its position on this or that or the other thing. And the maybe-this and maybe-that of conditionality will produce conditional Catholics, and conditional Catholics are deprived of the joy of unqualified discipleship. We are not dealing here with inconvenient rules of the Church that can be somehow changed at will. Again the words of *Familiaris Consortio:* "The Church is in no way the author or the arbiter of this norm," speaking about the nature of the conjugal act. "In obedience to the truth, which is Christ, whose image is reflected in the nature and dignity of the human person, the Church interprets the moral norm and proposes it to all people of good will without concealing its demands of radicality and perfection." The teaching of *Humanae Vitae* is illuminated by the more comprehensive argument of *Veritatis Splendor* in displaying an ensemble of mutually dependent insights that constitute the structure of faith regarding sexuality, marriage, and family.

"Commandments," says the Holy Father in *Veritatis Splendor,* "must not be understood as a minimum limit, not to be gone beyond, but rather as a path involving a moral and a spiritual journey toward perfection, at the heart of which is love (Col 3:14)" (*VS,* n. 15). It is pitiably inadequate to teach—and even this is not very consistently taught—that there are certain *Nos,* certain prohibitions, certain boundaries with respect to human behavior, also in sexuality, but every *No* is premised upon a greater *Yes.* And the great pastoral task is to propose the *Yes* in a way that is believable, the way of love that is openness to the other and openness to life, that is the uncompromised gift of the self to the other and ultimately to God. There are many of course who dismiss this as an impossible ideal. But you know—I trust you know—I certainly know married couples beyond numbering who live this way, and who love to tell us otherwise, that it is not an impossible ideal, that it is difficult. They testify that it is ideal and it is possible. We need more effectively to enlist their testimony in advancing the authentic sexual revolution, which is the liberation of sexuality from bondage to fear of life and bondage to the self. This too may be part of the springtime that we are called to anticipate, a world exhausted and disillusioned by the frenzied impossible demands of disordered desire, maybe ready, maybe even eager to hear the truth about love. But ready or not, it is the truth that we are commissioned to propose. In the past few years, of course, the credibility of the Church in the public arena, especially on questions of sexual morality, has taken a severe battering. How God will, as he certainly will, work renewal from the shambles that we have made of things and that the leadership of the Church has made of things, how exactly that will be done we don't know. But we know what it is that we must propose, that we have no choice but to persistently, winsomely, persuasively propose.

Well, *Familiaris Consortio,* long before the phrase "pro-family policy" was used in our politics, called for the politics of the family. The Holy Father pleaded with Catholics to become protagonists of family politics, directing our attention to the Church's charter of family rights,[3] a document that, I'm afraid, has almost been forgotten over the past decades since it was issued, in many ways a path-breaking document in its comprehensiveness and thoroughness and attractive presentation. The charter of family rights urged upon us the rich doctrine of subsidiarity, with specific relevance to family policy. No other state, no other party, no other academic institution, no other community of faith has proposed, possesses, or has composed such a compelling vision of the family in the modern world. That is a true statement, a bold proposal for family justice that can inform public thought and action on everything from welfare policy and employment practices to the right of parents to choose the education they want for their children. School choice has to be very close to the heart of the Church's proposal, for it is a matter of elementary justice, and for the poor among us it is increasingly a matter of survival.

And of course family rights presuppose the most primordial of rights, the right to life. To strike at the transmission of life is to strike at the heart of the family. Here, however inadequately, the Catholic Church has already had a transformative influence on our culture. And January 23, 1973, one day after the infamous *Roe v. Wade* decision, the *New York Times* declared, and all the network news stations declared, that the Supreme Court had, quote, "settled the abortion question." And here we are, thirty plus years later, and there's no more unsettled question in our public life, for which we ought to be profoundly grateful. We should recognize that there was only one major institution in January of 1973 that was in dissent from an otherwise unanimous, across-the-board agreement by all the culture-forming institutions in our society that were in support of what was then called liberalized abortion law. And that one institution in dissent was the Catholic Church. And however ineffective and however at times confused may have been the witness of the Church, it was

3. *Charter of the Rights of the Family,* presented by the Holy See to all Persons, Institutions and Authorities concerned with the Mission of the Family in Today's World (Rome: October 22, 1983).

that which prevented the complete triumph of the juggernaut of the ideology behind liberalized abortion, an ideology aptly described by the Holy Father and now understood by more and more people as being the culture of death. Without the Catholic Church there would be no pro-life movement in America or in the world today. Thank God we have many, many allies, but that truth remains. The proponents of abortion, of euthanasia, of population control, of cloning, of genetic engineering, of eugenics—they are all right to view the Catholic Church as the chief obstacle to their ambitions. We earnestly pray that one day they may be persuaded to be our friends, but until then we are grateful for their enmity.

So it is that we will not rest nor will we give others rest until every unborn child is a child protected in law and welcomed in life. We do not deceive ourselves about the encircling gloom of the culture of death; perhaps the darkness will grow still deeper—that's quite possible—but we will not despair. We have not the right to despair, and finally we have not the reason to despair, for we know that the light shines in the darkness and the darkness has not overcome it and never, never, ever will overcome it.

And so we come back to the opening statement, "Humanity's passage to the future is through the family." The prophetic humanism of John Paul II and of this Church proposes to the Catholic people and to the world how that future can be lived with moral dignity and even grandeur. We do not know, we can never know, how this proposal will be received, but we will persist in proposing it, in season and out of season. In the third millennium in its beginning, maybe it is a springtime at hand. Maybe the long dark winter, on the other hand, has just begun. We do not know. We do not need to know. God knows. But we know this: that now is the time of our testing, the time of our splendor in contending for the splendor of the truth, maybe the time of another second spring, for a faith that recognizes all times as springtime, if we have the will for it, and if we have the wit for it, and above all, if we have the faith for it.

six

~

Peter Kreeft
_____

JESUS' CONCEPT OF HAPPINESS

Two Meanings of "Happiness"

We must begin with the dullest but most necessary preliminary, that of defining our terms.

Nearly everyone, from Aristotle to Freud, agrees that we all seek happiness as our end. No one seeks it as a means to anything else. We argue about other objects of desire but not about happiness. We may argue, "What good are riches if they don't make you happy?" But we don't say "What good is happiness if it doesn't make you rich?"

This is clear to both ancients such as Aristotle and moderns such as Freud. But there is a very significant difference between the typically ancient and the typically modern meanings of "happiness." Ancient words for happiness, such as *eudaimonia* or *makarios* in Greek or *beatitudo* in Latin, mean "true, real blessedness," while the modern English word "happiness" usually means only subjective satisfaction or contentment; so that in modem English, if you feel happy you are happy, and it makes no sense to tell someone, "You feel happy, and you think you're happy, but you're not." Yet that saying is precisely the main point of the most famous book in the history of philosophy, Plato's *Republic:* that justice, the all-inclusive virtue, is always "profitable," that is, happifying, and injustice never is; that the just man, even if, like Socrates, he has nothing else, is happy, and the unjust man is not, even if he has everything else, like Gyges or Gollum with his magic ring of unlimited power and invisibility. Thus we must distinguish the ancient concept, which is really *blessedness,* from the modern, which is really *contentment.* I shall be dealing with *blessedness* here.

Blessedness differs from contentment in at least four ways, all of which can be seen by analyzing the Greek word *eudaimonia.*

It begins with the prefix *eu,* meaning "good," thus implying that you have to be good, especially morally good, to be happy.

Second, *daimon* means "spirit," thus implying that happiness is a matter of the soul rather than the body and its external goods of fortune. "Happiness," by contrast, comes from the Old English word *hap,* which means precisely fortune, luck, or chance—the one pagan thought-category that Christianity subtracted. (In all other cases, Christianity added to paganism. As Chesterton said, summarizing all spiritual history in three phrases: "Paganism was the biggest thing in the world, and Christianity was bigger, and everything since has been comparatively small.") If blessedness is spiritual, it is free. Thus we are responsible for our own blessedness, but "happiness" just "happens."

Third, *eudaimonia* ends in *-ia,* which means a lasting state, something permanent or whole. Contentment is only for the moment, blessedness is for a lifetime—so much so that Aristotle, in the *Nicomachean Ethics,* cannot make up his mind whether we should agree with the poet's dictum to "Call no man happy until he is dead," that is, "Wait for the end" of the story to judge it.

Fourth, and most important of all, the state of *eudaimonia* is an objective fact, while contentment is a subjective feeling.

When we say "happiness," we usually confuse these two meanings, the ancient and the modern. And that is not wholly unwise, because within the ancient concept of happiness (i.e., objectively real blessedness) there is also present in a secondary way the typically modern subjective ingredient, the need for contentment, peace of mind, some pleasure and not horrible pain, and at least a necessary modicum of the gifts of fortune; while within the modem concept of happiness (i.e., subjective contentment) we find implied the need for at least some virtue and the feeling that happiness, if it is to be deep and lasting, ought to be real, true happiness, whatever that is.

We are about to explore Christ's concept of happiness. It is typically ancient—*blessedness*—but it includes the above ambiguity, or double meaning, subjective satisfaction as well as objective perfection.

Our Concept of Happiness

When I speak of "our" concept of happiness, who is this "us"? I mean our culture, the mental landscape we all inhabit even when we feel like aliens here: most generally, the modem post-Christian West, but most specifically contemporary America as it would appear on opinion polls.

If an opinion poll were to ask Americans to list the nine most important ingredients in happiness, they would probably give an answer pretty much like the following.

The most obvious, though not the profoundest, ingredient would probably be money. If you notice your friend has a big smile on his face today, what is the commonest thing to say to him? "What happened to you? Did you just win the lottery?" If that's what you'd say, that's probably because that's what you think: that's what would put the biggest smile on *your* face. And let's face it, money can buy everything money can buy, and that isn't everything but it is a whole lot of Stuff.

Second might be freedom from pain. I think every one of us

would agree that the single most valuable invention in the history of technology has been anesthetics, once we try to imagine living in a world without them.

Third might be our culture's most notable success, the conquest of nature and fortune by science and technology, allowing each of us to be an Alexander the Great, a conqueror of the world.

Fourth might be self-esteem, the greatest good according to nearly all of our culture's new class of prophets, the secular psychologists. (And secular psychologists are among the most secular of all classes in our culture.)

Fifth might be justice, securing one's rights. "Justice and peace" summarize the social ideals of most Americans, the ideals they want for themselves and for the rest of the world.

Sixth, if we are honest, we'd have to include sex. To most Americans (unless they surf) this is the closest thing they can imagine to what we were most deeply designed for, namely heaven, that is, ecstasy, mystical experience, transcending the ego.

Seventh, we love to win—whether at war, at sports, at games of chance, in business, or in our fantasies. Our "positive self-esteem" requires the belief that we are "winners," not "losers." We want to be "successes," not "failures."

Eighth, we want honor. In most ancient societies one was honored for being different, better, superior, excellent. In our modem, egalitarian society we are honored not for being superior but for being one of the crowd. We want to be loved, accepted, and understood. But we still crave to be honored. Some even want to be famous. All want to be accepted.

Ninth, we want life, a long life and a healthy life. Hobbes is obviously right that fear of violent death, especially a painful and early death, is a very powerful motivator. Your life is hardly happy if your life is taken from you!

A Fantastic Thought-Experiment

This all seems so obvious and reasonable as to be beyond argument. Higher ideals than these are arguable—some seek them and some don't—but these nine would seem to be firm and impregnable, universal and necessary. Whoever would deny that they form a part of happiness would seem to be a fool. Whoever would affirm that happiness consisted in their opposites would seem to be insane.

Now let us perform a fantastic thought-experiment. Let us suppose that there was once a sage who did teach precisely that insanity, point for point, deliberately and specifically. Perhaps you cannot stretch your imagination that far, but I am going to ask you to stretch it even one step farther: imagine this man becoming the most famous, beloved, revered, respected, and influential teacher in human history. Imagine nearly everyone in the world, even those who did not classify themselves as his disciples, at least praising his wisdom, especially his moral wisdom, especially, the single most famous and beloved sermon he ever preached, the "Sermon on the Mount," the summary of his moral wisdom that begins with his 180-degree reversal of these nine truisms, which have been called the "beatitudes." Doubtless you find this fantasy far too fantastic to be even imaginable. It would be a miracle more difficult to believe than the idea of God becoming a man. It is hard enough to believe anyone actually believing the astonishing Christian claim that a certain man who began his life as a brainless embryo, then a sightless fetus, then a speechless baby, who would have died without his mother's milk, who did die on a cross executed as a criminal, and between birth and death got tired and hungry and angry and sad just like us—that this person is God, the eternal, beginningless, endless, infinitely perfect, all-wise, all-powerful creator of the universe. But it is even harder to believe that anyone would believe his utterly shocking paradoxes about happiness. Perhaps we don't really believe them after all; perhaps we only believe we believe them. Perhaps we have faith in faith rather than faith in him and his strange teachings.

The Beatitudes

The beatitudes are the most famous part of the most famous sermon in the most famous book in the world. They are the one part of the Bible still accepted by heretics, schismatics, apostates, dissenters, revisionists, nuancers, demythologizers, skeptics, modernists, liberals, and others who cannot quite bring themselves to believe all the other claims of the Bible or the Church. They truly strain at gnats but swallow the camel!

Let's look carefully at the camel they swallow. Perhaps they only seem to swallow it. Perhaps they swallow only their own swallowing, gulping like Gollum.

1. To our desire for wealth, Jesus says, "Blessed are the poor in spirit."

2. To our desire for painlessness, he says, "Blessed are those who mourn."

3. To our desire for conquest, he says, "Blessed are the meek."

4. To our desire for contentment and self-esteem, he says "Blessed are those who hunger and thirst for righteousness."

5. To our desire for justice, he says, "Blessed are the merciful."

6. To our desire for sexual pleasure, he says, "Blessed are the pure in heart."

7. To our desire for conquest, he says, "Blessed are the peacemakers."

8. To our desire for acceptance, he says, "Blessed are the persecuted."

9. To our desire for more life, he says, "Follow me"—to the Cross.

And this man, carrying his cross to Calvary, dares to tell us, "My yoke is easy and my burden is light."

Poverty

"Blessed are the poor in spirit, for theirs is the Kingdom of Heaven."

We say "How blessed we are" as a nation, a family, or an individual, when we have wealth. He says "No, you are blessed when you are poor—poor not only in your bank account but even more than that, poor in spirit, detached from riches, not even desiring riches, whether you have them or not."

"The poor in spirit," of course, do not mean the *weak*-spirited, but exactly the opposite: those strong enough in spirit to be detached from riches, that is, from the whole world that money can buy; those strong enough to be free from the slavery to their desires for the things of this world.

When Harvard University invited Mother Teresa to give its commencement address, she shocked them by taking issue with the invitation they sent to her, as the most well-known person in one of the world's poorest nations, to address people in the world's richest nation. She replied, "India is not a poor nation. India is a rich nation. She has a great variety of spiritual riches. And America is not a rich nation. America is a poor nation. America is a desperately poor nation. Any nation that slaughters her own unborn children is a desperately poor nation." And why are the babies killed? Because the mother fears that those children will be poor, or make her poor. She fears that she will not be able to "afford" these children. As if children were like cars, or computers: consumer goods rather than consumers, objects rather than subjects, calculable items in the household's economy.

The "insanity" of this beatitude turns out to be an illusion of perspective. In a lunatic asylum, from the lunatic's point of view, it is the sane outsider who is insane. How useful to have a supply of outsiders, Christ and his saints, to remind us where we live, how far east of Eden Bedlam is.

Mourning

"Blessed are those who mourn, for they shall be comforted."

What could Christ possibly mean by blessing mourners? Weeping is certainly not an expression of felt happiness, of contentment, of the painless state we all long for as part of happiness. Yet he tells us that mourners are blessed.

It is simply ridiculous for one Bible translation to translate *makarios* by "happy" here. To a society that means by "happy" simply "subjectively satisfied" or "content," it makes Christ say that those who weep are content, which is not a startling but meaningful paradox, but rather a meaningless self-contradiction.

Mourning is the expression of deep discontent, of the gap between desire and satisfaction, that is, of suffering. Buddha founded an entire religion on the problem of suffering *(dukkha),* its cause *(tanha,* selfish desire), and its cure (the noble eightfold path to *nirvana,* the "extinction" of the effect through the extinction of its cause). Unlike Buddha, Jesus came not to free us from suffering but to transform it, to make it salvific. He came to save us from sin, and he did that precisely by *embracing* suffering and death, which are the effects of sin. To say that suffering is redemptive must sound as absurd to a Buddhist as saying that sin is redemptive sounds to a Christian. Each religion must accuse the other of the most radical practical error, confusing the problem with the solution.

The reason Jesus gave for declaring mourners blessed is that "they shall be comforted"—completely, in the next life, but already in this life in hope. For hope makes the future present, hope lets the future cause changes in the present—not physically, but spiritually. Physically, you must put "one foot up and one foot down, that's the way to London Town" whether you are going to London Town to be crowned king or to be hanged in Traitor's Gate. But the future destiny of your journey makes all the difference to the journey itself, intrinsically and essentially, not just extrinsically or accidentally. A journey to be hanged is unblessed even if it is in the most comfortable coach; a journey to be crowned is blessed even if it is in the most uncomfortable wagon. St. Thérèse of Lisieux said that "all the way to heaven is heaven." St. Teresa of Avila said that the most horribly painful life on earth, looked at from the viewpoint of heaven, will seem like nothing more than one night in an inconvenient hotel. And Jesus has the viewpoint of heaven, and gives it to us. More, he gives heaven itself to us.

Meekness

"Blessed are the meek, for they shall inherit the earth."

The meek are not famous. The are *humble.* They do not thirst for honor, fame, or glory, and do not usually get it on earth. Yet they are blessed.

We all want to be known. That is natural. But if we are wise, we know that it is being known by God that blesses us, not being known by man. For "God knows the way of the righteous" (Ps 1), but not the way of the wicked. "The way of the righteous" is Christ himself: "I AM the Way" (Jn 14:6). To the damned he says, "Depart from me, I never knew you" (Mt 7.23).

Man's knowledge cannot bless us, St. Thomas notes, because it cannot change reality, only reflect it. But God's knowledge is creative, and life-changing. Our knowledge conforms to reality, but reality conforms to God's knowledge.

God, who is supremely blessed, is anonymous among us, hiding behind nature rather than bursting through miracles. He came here as a baby and died as a criminal. He lets himself be eaten daily as what looks like a little piece of bread. He is utterly meek, and utterly blessed. If we are utterly meek, we will be utterly blessed; if we are partly meek, we will be partly blessed; if we are not meek, we will not be blessed. For God is the source of all blessedness, and God is meek, and the effect cannot contradict the cause.

The meekness Christ calls blessed is in contrast not only to fame but also to power, to the desire to conquer nature that was Francis Bacon's new *summum bonum,* and the desire to conquer fortune that was Machiavelli's. But Christ is not here blessing wimps, sissies, dishrags, wallflowers, shrinking violets, worry warts, nebbishes, schlemiels, or Uriah Heeps. The meek are those who do not harm, those who do not see life as competitive because they understand the two premises from which this conclusion follows. The first is that the best things in life are not material things but spiritual things, that life's blessings are to be found in wisdom and love and creativity, understanding, and holiness and beauty, rather than money, power, fame, land, or military or athletic conquests. And the second premise is that spiritual things are not competitive, that they multiply when shared, while material things divide. So what sounds like nonsense is perfect logic:

Since happiness depends on understanding, seeking, and finding the best things in life;
And since the best things in life are spiritual;
And since spiritual things do not diminish when shared;
And since what does not diminish when shared cannot be attained by competition;
And since competition is the alternative to meekness;
Therefore meekness makes for happiness.

Christ the Logos is utterly logical.

But we aren't. That's why his pure reason sounds outrageously paradoxical to us: as Chesterton said, it is because we are standing on our heads, with our nose to the ground and our feet kicking up at the heavens. That's why Christ's philosophy seems upside down to us.

Hunger for Righteousness

*"Blessed are those who hunger and thirst for righteousness,
for they shall be filled."*

Christ's fourth beatitude cuts at the rotten flesh at the heart of our comfortable lives in this culture. And it shows us a striking difference between our culture and nearly all others, especially our own culture's past. As Solzhenitsyn said in his great Harvard commencement address in 1978, nothing is more conspicuous to an outsider than our lack of courage. We are not passionate. We are not even interesting.

Kierkegaard writes, in *Either/Or:*

> Let others complain that the age is wicked; my complaint is that it is wretched, for it lacks passion. Men's thoughts are thin and flimsy like lace, they are themselves pitiable like lace makers. The thoughts of their hearts are too paltry to be sinful. For a worm it might be regarded as a sin to harbor such thoughts, but not for a being made in the image of God. Their lusts are dull and sluggish, their passions sleepy. They do their duty, these shopkeeping souls, but they clip the coin a trifle . . . they think that even if the Lord keeps ever so careful a set of books, they may still cheat Him a little. Out upon them! This is the reason my soul always turns back to the Old Testament and to Shakespeare. I feel that those who speak there are at least human beings: they hate, they love, they murder their enemies, and curse their descendents throughout all generations, they sin.

The greatest good according to our culture's primary prophets, the secular psychologists, is self-esteem, self-satisfaction. Christ shocks us by blessing dissatisfaction: not the dissatisfaction with our place in the world, not worldly ambition, or "the profit motive," "the American Dream," hunger for wealth, fame, power, honor, glory, or "success," but hunger and thirst for righteousness, the demand to be a saint, the passionate dissatisfaction with our sins. If there is one thing in the lives of all the saints that bothers us the most it is their hatred of their sins.

Why don't we know, and love, and teach, the lives of the saints any more? It is perhaps the single most effective evangelistic weapon in the Church's arsenal. It's not that we don't admire saints, but that we don't hate sin, and we don't admire their hatred of sin, their passionate dissatisfaction with themselves, their discontent with their own righteousness. We are Pharisees. What Christ condemns, we bless; what he blesses, we condemn as "fanaticism"—our soft, sophisticated, sophistic culture's most deadly F-word. Our worst insult is his blessing. He demands that we be saints, that is, crazy people, fanatics, loving God with absolutely all of our heart and soul and mind and strength, putting all our eggs in his basket, selling everything for the one "pearl of great price." He used a shocking word for our Laodicean lukewarmness: "Because you are neither hot nor cold I will vomit you out of my mouth." He is content with us only if we are discontent with ourselves.

Freud said that our civilization's success in seeking contentment has produced instead greater discontent, but he did not know why. It was the profoundest thing he ever wrote (in *Civilization and Its Discontents*), only one step from Augustine's great answer, that our hearts are restless until they rest in God.

Pascal knew this. For Pascal's patient, unlike Freud's, was himself; and his psychoanalyst, unlike Freud's, was not himself but Christ. And therefore he knew why we multiply our diversions and our little passions for little things, and cultivate indifference to the greatest things, especially the four greatest things, the Four Last Things. He knew where this mental disease came from, writing in *Pensées:*

> The fact that there exist men who are indifferent to the loss of their being and the peril of an eternity of wretchedness is against nature. With everything else they are quite different: they fear the most trifling things, foresee and feel them . . . he knows he is going to lose everything through death but feels neither anxiety nor emotion. It is a monstrous thing to see one and the same heart at once so sensitive to minor things and so strangely insensitive to the greatest. It is an incomprehensible spell, a supernatural torpor that points to a supernatural power as its cause.[1]

Pascal wrote, "There are only three kinds of people: those who have sought God and found Him—and these are reasonable and happy; those who have sought God and have not yet found Him—and these are reasonable but unhappy; and those who neither seek God nor find

1. Blaise Pascal, *Pensées,* trans. A. J. Krailsheimer (London: Penguin Books, 1966).

Him—and these are both unhappy and unreasonable." It is the seeking, the thirsting, that makes all the difference, in fact the eternal difference.

Jesus was even more succinct than Pascal (Jesus was more succinct than anyone): "Seek and you shall find." Both Pascal and Jesus imply that nonseekers will never find.

Pharisees and pop psychologists are nonseekers. Both are too full of self-esteem. Jesus said to the Pharisees that he had come to earth to save everyone *but* them: "Those who are sick need a physician, but not those who are well. I came not to save the righteous, but sinners." To quote Pascal again: "There are two kinds of people: sinners, who believe they are saints, and saints, who know they are sinners." Socrates made the same judgment on the intellectual level: there are two kinds of people: fools, who think they are wise, and the wise, who know they are fools. Jesus says the saints and wise fools are right, and the clear test for the difference between the right and wrong is the hunger and thirst, the discontent, the passion.

When Christ says the hungerers for righteousness shall be satisfied, he obviously means the satisfaction of heaven, but I think he means that they will begin to be satisfied even here. The saints have a peace and a joy that the world simply cannot give. They are at the same time the most satisfied and the most dissatisfied, like lovers, like Romeo looking into Juliet's face, like listeners to a great symphony.

And by a wonderful paradox, the refusal to accept self-esteem turns out to be the very highest self-esteem. To accept the title "sinner" means that you are the King's kid acting like an ape. What a privilege to sing, "Amazing grace! How sweet the sound that saved a wretch like me!" No ape, however successfully evolved, can rise to the dignity of wretchedness. Only one destined for infinite, unending, and unimaginable ecstasy in spiritual marriage to infinite Beauty can bear the "weight of glory" of being wretched. Only the betrothed is wretched until united with the Spouse.

Mercy

"Blessed are the merciful, for they shall obtain mercy."

We want our rights. That's why we work for justice, for others' rights. We are practicing the Golden Rule. And this is justice. And it is good. But Christ does not call it "blessed." For justice is our minimum, not our maximum; our beginning, not our end; the foundation, not the house. Justice alone cannot ensure peace—in the world, in the family, or in friendships. Only mercy can. Our hope is not that we will receive justice in the end—what would become of us if we did? Our hope is "under the mercy." It was not justice but mercy that created us. (How could we justly deserve anything if we did not exist? And how could we deserve to be given existence if there was no we that existed yet?) It was mercy that redeemed us *from* the justice our sins deserved. And it is mercy that will gratuitously and graciously raise us higher than the sinless angels in uniting us with the divine nature. Christ did not become an angel, and no angel will become a cell in Christ's body.

Truth incarnate, who always meant exactly what he said, told us that "it is more blessed to give than to receive." Thus, the mere act of giving mercy is blessed. We do not give mercy only in order to get it, for that is justice, not mercy. We give mercy in order that the other may get it. And only thus, only by giving without the intention of getting, do we get mercy—not always from the person we give it to but always from God, who started the chain of mercy givers with the mercy of creation, restored it with the mercy of redemption, and will end it with the mercy of glorification. For the saved, the events in the Book of Revelation should not be called "the last judgment" but "the last mercy." For that is where it ends: "Let him who wills come and take the water of life without price."

God gives mercy, and God is blessed, and we are blessed by being Godlike, therefore we are blessed by giving mercy.

Purity of Heart

"Blessed are the pure of heart, for they shall see God."

When we hear the word "purity" we immediately think of sexual purity. Perhaps Christ had that primarily in mind, perhaps not; but our reaction tells us something significant about us, namely that sex is our new absolute, our society's new god. Anything will be done, tolerated, justified, sanctified, and glorified for this god. One-third of our mothers pay healers to murder their own unborn babies in sacrifice to this god, against nature's strongest instinct. (Of course abortion is about sex; the only reason for abortion is to have sex without live babies. Abortion is backup contraception.) Or look at our society's acceptance of divorce everywhere except in the Church. Families, the only absolutely necessary building blocks of all societies, are destroyed for this god. Half of America's new citizens commit suicide for this god, for divorce is the suicide of the new "one flesh" that love had created. No one justifies lying, cheating, betrayal, promise-breaking, or devastating and harming strangers; but we justify, we expect, we tolerate, doing all this to the one person you promise most seriously to be faithful to forever. No one justifies child abuse, except for sex. Divorce is child abuse for sex. Even all the churches accept it, claiming the authority to correct Christ, who clearly forbade divorce in all four Gospels—all the churches except the one Church that is accused of being "authoritarian."

Why is purity of heart blessed? It doesn't seem to be. Because lust gives such an immediate thrill of delight, this beatitude too seems paradoxical. But anything natural is happier, more blessed, in its pure, natural condition. St. Thomas deduces from this principle that sexual pleasure was far greater before the Fall.

When he specifies the reward as "seeing God," he does not mean merely in the next life, getting box seats instead of bleacher seats in heaven's stadium as a just reward for paying more for the tickets here. The reward is experienced in this life too. St. Thomas himself exemplified it. His wonderful clarity of mind came partly from the fact that he was never troubled by this universal albatross of concupiscence, because God gave him a supernatural gift of purity of heart at one specific time in his life, when he resisted his brothers' attempt to seduce him out of the Dominicans by a prostitute. His mind was free from his passions, free for the high vocation God planned for him. Christ says, to the Jews who ask him how they can understand his teaching, "If your will were to do the will of my Father, you would understand my teaching." Purity of will produces the purity of mind that understands God.

Most of the Doctors of the Church, including Augustine and Aquinas, locate the chief harm in lust in its blinding of the reason, the narrowing and skewering of perspective. The fact that we are surprised at this says more about us than about them.

Surely there is a connection between the impurity of the desires of most modern students and the impurity of their motivation for education; between the decline of the pure sexual love of the other for the sake of the other and the decline of the pure intellectual love of the truth for the sake of the truth; between the contemplative wonder and respect toward the body's mate and toward the mind's. To love truth not for its own sake but for some further personal, instrumental, pragmatic, utilitarian end is a form of impurity of heart, a sort of intellectual prostitution. And it has polluted modern philosophy since Bacon.

The blessing Christ promises here is verifiable in this life, in experience, though perfected only in the next. I wonder how many theologians fail to "see" God, understand God purely, because of impure desires? Almost all theological "dissent" today, amazingly, stems from or leads to dissent about sexual morality. It looks suspiciously like addicts obsessing about their drug and not really caring about much else. Perhaps that's why most homilies and catechisms are so bland and passionless. Why else do we *never* hear a homily on sexual morality, even though that is the single most divisive and controversial issue in our Church and in our culture? Perhaps that's why our children are so theologically undernourished: because there is something missing in the hearts of their educators, the writers of those stunningly dull CCD and RCIA texts. Perhaps the blood that their hearts pump into their brains is diluted with fluids from other organs. Perhaps our liturgical language and our liturgical music are so dumbed down and dull, so embarrassingly wimpy, for reasons much more psychological than musicological. Limp liturgies come from limp liturgists. There should be no need to even mention the current clerical scandals. (I hear a single syllable echoing everywhere: "DUH.")

Peacemaking

"Blessed are the peacemakers, for they shall be called the sons of God."

Christ blesses peacemakers, not just peace. Peacemakers are not pacifists. Peacemakers are warriors, spiritual warriors, warriors against war. Sometimes war can be conquered only by war. Everyone speaks highly of peacemaking, so how is this beatitude countercultural to anyone but terrorists? Because the peace Christ blesses is the peace the world cannot give: peace with neighbor, self, and God, not with the world, the flesh, and the devil. It is a peace that comes with the three countercultural virtues of poverty, chastity, and obedience, not a peace with greed, lust, and pride. The two kinds of peace, in fact, are at war with each other. Many of our world's peacemakers will embrace Christ's peace, but only if they do not have to give up the world's peace, only if they do not have to fight and sacrifice for it. Thus, paradoxically, we lack peace because we are reluctant to war against the enemies of peace.

We also lack peace because we do not rightly order its three dimensions. We preach incessantly about peace with neighbor, but seldom about peace with God. But surely Thomas Merton was profoundly right when he diagnosed all our ills in two sentences: "We are not at peace with each other because we are not at peace with ourselves. And we are not at peace with ourselves because we are not at peace with God." Christ did the same, in putting the first table of the law first, as Moses did. We need to relearn lesson one.

The world accuses Christianity of being negative, repressive, and judgmental rather than peaceful. They are half right: it is those three things, but that does not make it the enemy of peace. Christianity announces to our sleeping souls that we are at war, ever since a certain incident with a serpent, and war necessarily judges the enemy. That's why a war is fought: because a judgment is made about an enemy. War is also repressive, for it tries to repress the enemy. That is what defense is: repressing the enemy's offence. And war is negative, for its offense tries to negate the enemy's defense. Our enemies are just as real as flesh and blood, though they are not flesh and blood but principalities and powers, evil spirits. Our enemies are also our own sins. Our commanding officer told us that he came into this world to bring a sword to wage and win this war. His sword is a cross, which he uses like a syringe, to give us a blood transfusion from his own body. It is the exact opposite of Dracula, who, like the demons, takes our blood, our life. We are in the middle of a battlefield between Christ and Antichrist, Christ and Dracula, Christ and demons. That is why Christ blesses not pacifism but peacemaking, which is done only by waging and winning a spiritual war on the enemies of peace.

When Christ says that peacemakers are blessed because they "will be called the sons of God," he does not mean that peacemaking is the cause and being a son of God is the effect. Rather, only sons of God can make God's peace. Peacemaking is the effect of the divine life (sanctifying grace, the new birth, regeneration, supernatural life, theosis), and peacemakers are called sons of God, known to be sons of God, because we know the cause from the effect.

Persecution

"Blessed are you when men persecute you . . . for yours is the Kingdom of Heaven."

The eighth beatitude blesses not just pain and suffering but being persecuted, that is, suffering imposed by rejection and hatred. This is the only one of the eight beatitudes that Christ repeats, emphasizing it as the final and most outrageous beatitude of all.

Everyone wants to be loved. How can it be blessed to be hated? One possible explanation is utterly inconsistent with Christ: a detached, sneering superiority, as if it were blessed to say to those who hate us, "We wouldn't want love from damned fools and worthless scum like you." Surely it is great grief that the persecutors are fools, and infinitely grievous that they, or anyone, may be damned. (Of course they are not worthless scum; if they were, there would be no reason for our grief for them.) We grieve for their unblessed state if we love them, as we are commanded to do, as Christ loved and grieved for those who killed him, and prayed for them.

Note how easy two alternatives are. It is easy for us to hate our enemies, and it is also easy for us to say that there is nothing to forgive and that to the enlightened mind there are no such things as enemies. But Christ does not say "Do not say 'enemies'; it is not nice." He commands us to love them. (Of course, the love that can be commanded is not desire, or feeling, or instinct, or attitude, but practical charity, willing the good of the other with both will and actions.)

The reward that makes being persecuted blessed is the same as the one that makes poverty blessed: the kingdom of Heaven. Persecution has the same blessing as poverty because it is a form of poverty; it is the poverty of love rather than the poverty of money. It is the poverty or lack not of loving but of being loved.

We desperately crave love from the world. But the world is not God. The world is fallen. The world is therefore afraid of Christ, as the cavity is afraid of the dentist, as the liar is afraid of the light. (I use "world" here in the New Testament sense: not the planet *(gaia),* not the matter God created and declared good, but the era *(aion)* of sin and the world-order of "the prince of this world.")

Persecution is not blessed in itself but only because it is "for righteousness' sake." If we are persecuted for being righteous, we are persecuted for God's sake, for being what God is. The righteous pagan such as Socrates is also blessed when he is misunderstood, rejected, hated, persecuted, and martyred.

Just as your peacemaking is a sign that you are a child of God, and thus blessed, so being persecuted for the sake of righteousness is also a sign that you are a member of God's kingdom and thus blessed. Blessing comes only from what is good, and persecution, poverty, and the like are not good in themselves. Christ is not a Stoic or a Hindu or a Buddhist; blessing does not come from apathy or indifference to the good things of the world that God created; or from seeing through this world as maya, illusion; or from the spiritual euthanasia that kills the patient to cure the disease, that kills our desires so that we can avoid the suffering they bring. Christians know something real and good that Stoics, Hindus, and Buddhists do not know (even though they may implicitly long for it and attain it in the end). That something is, simply, Jesus Christ, the *summum bonum,* the total good, human and divine in one. It is he who makes blessed even the nails in the cross. And it is *only* he.

Death

"He that loses his life for my sake shall find it."

Our ninth natural desire is life, and the ninth beatitude is death. Death contains all the other losses, and, paradoxically, all the other blessings. Christ teaches us the blessing of death not in words, like the other eight blessings, but in deed, by the cross.

The cross reveals the hidden source of all eight blessings: the historical fact (not an abstract philosophical principle, which has no power to change things) that God, out of sheer love, became incarnate, died, and rose to save us from sin and death and hell. As Dorothy Sayers put it, "the dogma is the drama." By this dramatic judo, death itself was turned into an instrument for life, as an earthen dam is so overwhelmed by the waters of the flood that conquers it that the dam is swept along and made into a part of the flood itself. So the flood of God's infinite life of unstoppable love, when it entered our world, not only conquered death but turned death into life's most powerful instrument. In the words of an old oratorio significantly titled "Open Our Eyes," "Thou hast made death glorious and triumphant, for through its portals we enter into the presence of the Living God."

We anticipate that final death, and its final blessing, in all our little deaths now, by our participation in Christ's other eight beatitudes. We not only anticipate it, we actually participate in it, in these real little (or large) dyings. And we also both anticipate and participate in the final blessing, "the presence of the Living God," every time we "open our eyes" and see *Who* it is that is really present there, where our half-closed eyes see only the most undramatic little round wafer of bread. How absurd that we find it easy to get up off our knees!

The secret of happiness is Jesus. Not the philosophy of Jesus but Jesus, his real presence. He actually comes to us in such unlikely vehicles as poverty, pain, and persecution. He has weird taste in vehicles. He came to Jerusalem on an ass. He comes to us also on similar beasts: each other.

And where he comes, he acts. He acts with power but also with subtlety rather than bombast, like a tide slowly and irresistibly flooding the land rather than like a storm suddenly smashing into it. But the difference he makes is palpable. I am haunted by my memories of the two happiest groups of people I have ever met. One was a community of cloistered contemplative Carmelite nuns, in Danvers, Massachusetts. The other was a community of Mother Teresa's Missionaries of Charity, in Boston's worst slum. In both cases I was supposed to speak to them. Whatever I said, it was very little compared with what they said to me, simply by being who they were: "See how happy Jesus makes us!" This is how happiness happens: it is not taught, like math, but caught, like measles. The Church is in the business of spreading the good infection. Ever since the Incarnation God's secret plot for world history has been "the invasion of the body snatchers," not to dehumanize but to humanize and to divinize, to incorporate into Christ and therefore into happiness.

This is "the new evangelism"—and also the old evangelism that won the world two millennia ago. It will do it again, for there is no argument against real happiness. The smiles of saints are unconquerable arguments. There is only "one thing necessary" to create a world of happiness, a smile from pole to pole. It is any of the many good things Martha did, but the one thing Mary did: sitting at Jesus' feet, being in his presence, all day, with all your heart. That is the scandalously simple secret of happiness.

seven

John Haas

CHRIST, THE REDEEMER OF CULTURE

One of the principal characteristics of the pontificate of Pope John Paul II was his repeated calls for the re-evangelization of culture, sometimes just known as the New Evangelization. It seems that there was not an encyclical, an apostolic exhortation, or a *motu proprio* that did not contain a call for a New Evangelization. But what is meant by this?

It is surely and most fundamentally what is written in Scripture: "Be not conformed to this world, but be transformed by the mind of Christ." We know how much the world is in need of transformation, from individual lives to its most complex social institutions. When the Holy Father was in Los Angeles, during his second pastoral visit to the United States, he asked, "But how is American culture evolving today? Does it clearly reflect Christian inspiration? Your music, your poetry and art, your drama, your painting and sculpture, the literature that you are producing, are all those things which reflect the soul of a nation being influenced by the spirit of Christ for the perfection of humanity?"[1]

In that remarkable quotation, John Paul provided the most succinct definition of culture one could imagine. Culture is all "those things which reflect the soul of a nation."[2] And Pope John Paul wanted to know if all of these things which reflect the soul of a nation were being influenced by the Spirit of Christ. But we must then ask, "Toward what end?" Why do we want culture to be influenced by the Spirit of Christ?

The Holy Father answered the question himself: we Catholics desire that culture be influenced by the Spirit of Christ "for the perfection of humanity." The pope's call for the evangelization of culture has nothing to do with a desire to establish a Western culture of hegemony over other people. It is not a papal call for some Christian version of a holy jihad. It is a call to allow the spirit of Christ to pervade and permeate society through the lives of those who are conformed to him in baptism, to live his life in the world. Why do we look to Jesus for this? We are told in the *Pastoral Constitution on the Church in the Modern World,* "The truth is that only in the mystery of the Incarnate Word does the mystery of man take on light."[3]

We are accustomed to hearing about the "mystery of God" taking on light in the Incarnate Word, but the council tells us here the "mystery of man" takes on light. "For Adam, the first man, was a figure of him who was to come, namely Christ the Lord. Christ, the final Adam, by the Revelation of the mystery of the Father and his love, fully reveals man to man himself, and makes his supreme calling clear."[4]

If we would know how human persons are to live, we look to Jesus Christ. And in him, we see a man who was entirely for others. That is

---

1. National Catholic News Service, *Pope John Paul II "Building up the Body of Christ": Pastoral Visit to the United States* (San Francisco: Ignatius Press, 1987), 188.

2. Ibid.

3. Vatican Council II, *Gaudium et Spes* (Dogmatic Constitution on the Church in the Modern World, December 7, 1965), n. 22.

4. Ibid.

why he came: to serve and not to be served. He came to do the will of his Father. It was with that attitude, and in a life of service to others, that Christ gave us the key to human happiness. For as the council said, "He reveals to us, not only God, but also what it is to be man." In his encyclical *The Gospel of Life,* the pope repeats Ezekiel's promise that we will be given a new heart. This new heart, the pope tells us, "will make it possible to appreciate and achieve the deepest and most authentic meaning of life, namely that of being a gift which is fully realized in the giving of self."[5] This indeed is the key to human happiness, "being a gift which is fully realized in the giving of self."

The theologian Augustine DiNoia, OP, said once, "People are afraid to give of themselves, as Christ gave us the example." He pointed out that it seems counterintuitive to think that we *gain* the most by *giving* of ourselves. He captured the reticence of anyone to embrace Christ's message when he said, "We have to realize that dying to self is not fatal."[6] That is the problem with humanity in its fallen condition: people think they will be diminished, they will cease to be, if they die to self; yet it is in so doing that we receive the fullness of life.

Now we know that Catholicism is perceived by many not as an institution that gives of itself fully for others. It is seen by many as being anticultural, as being repressive, as being intolerant. We see these notions expressed from the purported high culture of the university classroom to the low pop culture of the movie theater. The movie *Robin Hood* was released a number of years ago. Even in what should have been a perfectly innocuous film there were anti-Catholic elements. Early in the film, Robin encounters a black Moor, with whom he becomes a fast friend. And in a manner that we have come to expect of fashionable prejudice, worthy of the Enlightenment, Christianity is compared unfavorably with Islam. Christianity is portrayed as being intolerant and violent. As Robin Hood kneels in grief at the

---

5. John Paul II, *Evangelium Vitae (EV)* (Encyclical on the Value and Inviolability of Human Life, March 25, 1995), n. 49.

6. Augustine DiNoia, OP, in a lecture attended by the author.

grave of his father, who was killed by the wicked Sheriff of Notting-ham, he remembers his father trying to dissuade him from joining the Crusades. And he says to the Moor, speaking of his father, "He called the Crusades a foolish quest. He said it was vanity to force men to our religion."

How many millions of children sat there and just picked up this type of subtle anti-Catholic attitude? We all know that the Cru-sades were not about forcing anybody to accept our religion. For all the horrors that attend even the most just military campaigns—and there were certainly enough that accompanied the Crusades—they were fundamentally about securing access for Christians to the Holy Lands and to the holy shrines and providing Christians with protec-tion from Islamic harassment. The truth of the matter, as we all know, is that Islam swept over Christian North Africa and the Middle East, obliterating the religion of the Nazarene and forcefully denying his followers access to the most holy sites of their faith. It is to this intol-erant and often fanatical religion that the Holy Father referred in his address to the United Nations on October 6, 1995. "Nationalism," he said, "particularly in its most radical forms, is thus the antithesis of true patriotism, and today we must ensure that extreme nationalism does not continue to give rise to new forms of the aberrations of to-talitarianism."[7]

"This is a commitment which also holds true," he said, "obviously in cases where religion itself is made the basis of nationalism, as un-fortunately happens in certain manifestations of so-called fundamen-talism."[8] We know what he was addressing. We know that the Cru-sades were driven by an ardent desire for religious freedom, and it is out of this historical memory that the leadership of the Catholic Church, even now, calls for an international status for the most holy city of Jerusalem. Nothing so moves a people as their religious beliefs, the foundation of any culture.

7. John Paul II, Address of His Holiness to the Fiftieth General Assembly of the United Nations Organization, New York (October 5, 1995), n. 11.

8. Ibid.

We know that the root word for culture is *cultus,* the Latin for worship. Fundamentally, the forces giving rise to "all those things which
reflect the soul of a nation," are religious. They reflect what constitutes the basic religious orientation of a people, what the Protestant
theologian Paul Tillich called our "ultimate concern."[9] Consequently,
it is not a matter of indifference which religious inspiration is shaping
our culture. The differences in societies that have been shaped by the
Gospel and those shaped by the Koran are stark: the status of wom-
en, the respect shown to the religious beliefs of others, national traits
of tolerance, respect for human dignity. Ironically, in our own country, and also in other countries that traditionally have been shaped by
the Christian message, it is becoming increasingly difficult to preach
the Gospel. It becomes almost impossible for the good news of Jesus
Christ, as it is preached in its fullness by the Catholic Church, to be
heard. And if the Gospel cannot be heard, if it cannot be appropriat-
ed, it cannot redeem; it cannot transform culture.

It is not merely false societal perceptions of what Catholics actually believe and practice that make that transformation difficult in this
country. In a way there are even deeper, more profound factors making it almost impossible for the Catholic message to be heard. There
are distorted ideas about the world and the human person in our society, antithetical to the Christian message, that have become the very
cultural lenses through which we view reality.

We can, perhaps, speak of certain cultural coordinates, which enable societies and individuals to negotiate their ways through normal
as well as chaotic times. As you know, in mathematics, coordinates
are any of the fixed magnitudes that define the position of a point or
a line by reference to a fixed figure. Coordinates serve a similar role
in sailing. The sailor takes his coordinates from the fixed night sky so
that he may successfully navigate to his destination. Likewise, there
are certain cultural coordinates, certain ideas and concepts, that seem
unalterably fixed. One does not call them into question, because one

9. Paul Tillich, *Dynamics of Faith* (New York: Harper and Brothers, 1957), chapter 1, part 1.

could not imagine navigating one's way through life without them. However, we know that if one chooses the wrong star as one of his coordinates, he may never reach his destination.

We are living in difficult times. In his magnificent encyclical *Evangelium Vitae,* Pope John Paul II warned us that we live in a time of "the most alarming corruption and the darkest moral blindness."[10] And it is not simply wicked men doing wicked deeds, but entire societies misunderstanding the nature of the human person and consequently forging social policies that are profoundly threatening to individual and social well-being. In *Reconciliatio et Paenitentia,* the pope pointed out that "it happens not infrequently in human history for more or less lengthy periods and under the influence of different factors that the moral conscience of many people becomes seriously clouded."[11] And this has happened in our own society.

Again in *Evangelium Vitae,* Pope John Paul spoke of "attacks affecting life in its earliest and in its final stages, attacks which present new characteristics with respect to the past and which raise questions of extraordinary seriousness. It is not only that in generalized opinion these tend no longer to be considered as crimes," which they had been throughout most of Western history. "Paradoxically," the pope said, "they assume the nature of rights, to the point that the state is called upon to give them legal recognition and to make them available through the free health serves of health care professionals."[12] He laments that we have come "to interpret crimes against life as legitimate expressions of individual freedom to be acknowledged and protected as actual rights."[13] One almost senses the bewilderment of the pope as he reflects on this profound and regrettable shift in cultural attitudes where actions, which two generations ago were unspeakable crimes, are now hailed as rights.

10. *EV,* n. 24.
11. John Paul II, *Reconciliatio et Paenitentia* (Apostolic Exhortation, December 2, 1984), n. 18.
12. *EV,* n. 11.
13. Ibid., n. 18.

When teaching at Saint Charles Borremeo Seminary, I was talking to an older secretary who was about to retire. She spoke of having gone out into the workforce right after the Second World War. She remembered sitting in church one Sunday as the priest talked about the changes in societal attitudes that were coming about because of the disruptions of the war. She said she remembered vividly that he had said that if trends continued as they were going, there might come the day in our country when abortion would be legal. She said, "When I heard that word 'abortion' uttered from the pulpit, I became nauseous."

So unspeakable was the thought of abortion that this good young woman became nauseous at the mere mention of the word. And then decades later the Clinton administration actually tried to force countries that still had laws protecting the unborn to abrogate those laws, acting as though women had innate natural rights to kill the children they would carry within their womb. John Paul II went on in the *Gospel of Life* to ask how such a situation could have come about.

Many looked on this encyclical as a significant development in moral thought. However, it was not. How does one advance on the commandment "Thou shalt do no murder"? One cannot. It is written on the hearts of men, as St. Paul said. Rather, that encyclical was a profound critique of modern culture. In it, John Paul answered the question how one-time murderous deeds could come to be viewed as rights. He wrote, "In the background there is the profound crisis of culture which generates skepticism in relation to the very foundations of knowledge and ethics and which makes it increasingly difficult to grasp clearly the meaning of what man is, the meaning of his rights and duties."[14]

Catholics must realize that the culture within which they find themselves in the United States is overwhelming guided by "coordinates" that are not Catholic and indeed that militate against the perfection of humanity of which the pope spoke in Los Angeles. The cultural coordinates in the United States, which guide our social lives,

14. Ibid., n. 11.

our individual lives, and increasingly even the life of the institutional Catholic Church, are fundamentally Protestant and/or secular. Consequently, Catholic teaching itself has come to be seen through the lenses of the dominant Protestant or secular culture.

Catholics may constitute the largest religious body in this country, with more than 64 million members. The next largest religious group is the Baptists, with 12 million. However, collectively the Protestants outnumber Catholics, and their understandings of religion and of man are the ones that are dominant. Increasingly, in the United States Catholics themselves come to understand their own faith more within the Protestants' fundamental beliefs than within a Catholic cultural context, which would sustain and elucidate Catholic teaching. And this has been of no little significance in the emergence of the modern phenomenon of theological dissent in the Church.

Pope John Paul complained of this development when he said, "It is no longer a matter of limited and occasional dissent, but of an overall and systematic calling into question of traditional moral doctrine, on the basis of certain anthropological and ethical presuppositions."[15] Once again we are taken back to the cultural problem: at the root of the presuppositions are the more or the less obvious currents of thought that end by detaching human freedom from its essential and constitutive relationship to truth. Contemporary society supposes one can have freedom without truth. The contribution of Protestant thought to this situation, mediated through cultural presuppositions and practices, can hardly be minimized. It is admittedly very difficult to speak in general terms of Protestantism, since there are so many different beliefs found among its various groups, but there are certain general doctrines associated with its principal leaders, specifically Martin Luther and John Calvin, that can be identified.

One can see in the classical sixteenth-century formulations of Protestant thought elements that have contributed to the cultural crisis of

---

15. John Paul II, *Veritatis Splendor* (Encyclical, August 6, 1993), n. 4.

which the Holy Father speaks. They have contributed to the detaching of human freedom from its essential and constructive relationship to truth. It is the intellect, of course, that brings us into contact with reality itself. "Truth," St. Thomas reminds us, "is the conformity of mind to reality."[16] But the Protestant doctrine of the total depravity of man renders the intellect not only an uncertain guide, but a fatally dangerous one. Man's corruption is so profound, so deep, that there is nothing that is not infected by it. Even when man is, in Luther's formula, justified by grace through faith alone, he remains thoroughly corrupt. Righteousness, within the Protestant scheme, is imputed to the sinful man.

The sinful man does not become righteous; he is merely counted as righteous. He remains *simul justus et peccator:* at one and the same time a most vile sinner, even while God treats him as though he were just. When God looks at the sinner, and this is Luther's own metaphor, he sees not the sinner, but rather Jesus Christ, within whom the sinner has cloaked himself. So God imputes the righteousness of Christ to man, and this is what constitutes his salvation. Another image of Luther's that may be familiar is that of the pile of dung in the barnyard, covered with a layer of glistening white snow. Luther said when one goes and wipes away the white snow what one has is the same smelly dung that was there before the snow fell upon it. Look beneath the cloak of Jesus Christ, and the dung is all too evident.

The intellect, along with all the other faculties and appetites of man, remains totally corrupt. It cannot be trusted to obtain truth. Philosophy is a dangerous enterprise, leading us to perdition by suggesting that there is some trustworthy good in our intellect. Aristotle, if you remember, is dismissed by Luther as that babbling buffoon who has misled the Church. Reason is "the devil's whore,"[17] always ready to

16. St. Thomas Aquinas, *Summa theologiae* Ia, q. 16.

17. Martin Luther, "Last Sermon in Wittenberg, Second Sunday in Epiphany, 17 January 1546," in *Dr. Martin Luther's Werke: Kritsche Gesamtsusgabe* (Weimar, Germany: Herman Boehlaus Nachfolger, 1914), 51:126.

seduce us to our ruin. If one is to be saved, Luther tells us in his commentary on Paul's letter to the Galatians, every Christian must act as the true priest that he is, for first he offers up and kills his own reason. We are to offer up our reason as the evening sacrifice, according to Luther.[18]

The great German phenomenologist of religion in the first half of the last century, Rudolph Otto, purported merely to describe religious phenomena in his classic work *The Idea of the Holy*. But of course, he cannot do so outside his own cultural milieu, and he was a German Lutheran. So when he looks for that singular characteristic of the human experience of the divine, it is of the "irrational." His book *Das Heilige* was translated into English simply as *The Idea of the Holy*. In the German, the subtitle is *Über das Irrationale in der Idee des Göttlichen: Concerning the Irrational in the Idea of the Holy and Its Relation to the Rational*. The Catholic will certainly acknowledge the reality of the complete otherness of God, and therefore what appears at times as arbitrary actions of his. But the Catholic struggles to understand them and would see them as perhaps suprarational, but certainly not irrational. God is not in opposition to human reason, but rather ineffably surpasses it.

Also, the Protestant principle of *sola scriptora* is linked to the private interpretation of Scripture and has surely been one of the most powerful cultural impetuses toward the widespread subjectivism of our day. This doctrine is sometimes called the "internal testimony of the Holy Spirit." The *Westminster Confession* states succinctly, "Our full persuasion and assurance of the infallible truth and divine authority of scripture is from the inward work of the Holy Spirit bearing witness by and with the Word in our hearts."[19] Calvin described this inner assurance as "a conviction that requires no reasons."[20] Without

---

18. John Dillenberger, ed., *Martin Luther: Selections from His Writings* (Garden City, N.J.: Anchor Books, 1961), 131.

19. *Westminster Confession,* chapter I, n. 5.

20. John Calvin, *Institutes of the Christian Religion,* I. vii. 4.

reasons, of course, there is no role for reason. Protestants have always made appeal to the certitude that they have interiorly to the convictions they hold, even when these convictions separate them from the testimony and fellowship of other Christians, and indeed of the entire Christian tradition that had preceded them. They allow no authority, other than their own, to judge the correctness or error of their belief.

The Catholic avoids subjectivism by always receiving his beliefs from the community of Faith and by having his interpretation of Scripture measured against the common Faith of the community and the authoritative teaching of the Magisterium. In Luther's mind, no reliance could be placed on the Magisterium of the Church. The Church is simply the congregation of likeminded individuals called together by God. Luther repudiated an authoritative teaching body within, and at the service of, the Church. He asks in derisive mocking, "Tell me, dear pope, what is the Church? Answer: The pope and his cardinals. Oh listen to that, you dunce, where is it written in God's word that father pope and brother cardinal are the true church? Was it because that was what the fine parrot bird said to the black jackdaw?"[21]

One does not often read these quotes from Luther in the theological textbooks, but he had colorful ways of expressing himself. According to Luther, Church authority has allowed "the miserable pope and his decretals to make of the Church of God a filthy privy."[22] Such a rejection of external authority goes hand in hand, of course, with the doctrine of total depravity. Human reason, human will, human agencies, human institutions, human agents, acting for God—are all suspect. Humanity itself becomes suspect.

Calvin's view of human imperfection is attributed to man even prior to the Fall. This admittedly betrays a shocking tendency toward Gnosticism, the early heresy of the Church that viewed material creation itself as fallen and corrupt. The human body was a prison for man's true nature, which was spiritual and divine. To paraphrase Cal-

21. Dillenberger, *Martin Luther,* 247.
22. Ibid., 248.

vin, even if man had remained in his integrity, still his condition was too base for him to attain to God; how much less could he have raised himself so far after staining himself with so many defilements, nay even stinking in his corruption and overwhelmed with misery. The image of God has become so deeply corrupted that all that remains of it is a horrible deformity, so that man can do no more than crawl over the earth like little worms.[23]

It is not just the faculty of reason that has been totally corrupted, or course, but also that other great spiritual faculty of man, the will. Luther wrote his treatise on the *Bondage of the Will* against the claims of the great Catholic humanist Erasmus, who argued that the will was free. Calvin's radical doctrine of double predestination, by which God has destined men to heaven or hell before they are born, no matter what they may do, also provides an understanding of the human person that is radically at odds with a Catholic one. Such understandings of the human person have contributed mightily to both the belief in determinism and the cult of absolute freedom, which are such dominant characteristics of our culture and to which John Paul referred when he spoke of our cultural crisis. The psychological determinist B. F. Skinner wrote his own treatise on the bondage of the will for our own day and entitled it *Beyond Freedom and Dignity*. Freudian analysts, likewise, see us captive to unconscious libidinal drives and subconscious attempts to settle unresolved conflicts buried deeply in our childhood if not our infancy. They might say: "Oh, you think you became a clarinetist because you love music, and cherish the timbre and sonorous tones of your instrument; however, your mother weaned you too early and you spend your life seeking to resolve the tensions and conflicts that resulted from your being deprived of adequate gratification of your drive for pleasure during the oral stage of your psychosexual development."

These underlying cultural determinants have many and varied

---

23. Calvin, *Institutes of Christian Religion,* book 1.

manifestations, but they all tend to diminish a sense of culpability and personal responsibility for one's actions and therefore of morality itself. If one is saved by grace alone without any human cooperation and if all action is tainted with sin, one can simply, indeed one must, as Luther put it, sin boldly. There comes to be a great divide between the interior life of the spirit and the external actions that are performed. Those actions need not conform to any objective standards of human nature since that nature is thoroughly corrupt, as is our attempt to see and understand it. Since man cannot know the truth of things and cannot be trusted to formulate appropriate courses of action to help him attain his goal, he must rely on someone showing him the way; he relies on the lawgiver.

Thus the Protestant approach to morality tends to be voluntarist and legalistic. If man cannot rely on reason, he must look to the law, as it is given to him and as it reflects the will of the lawgiver. Protestantism develops a morality of the book.

How do we know that adultery is wrong, that we ought not do it? The Ten Commandments in the Bible tell us so, and they reflect the mind of the Divine Lawgiver. The law has its grounding not in divine reason, but in the divine will. Again we see such cultural presuppositions in the high culture of our university law schools and the reigning legal positivism in our country. The law becomes fundamentally arbitrary. Its force derives from the will of authority, from the *arbitrium*. This shapes the way our culture views morality. It is fundamentally legalistic. It can be seen in the way the popular perception of abortion changed over time after the Supreme Court ruling of *Roe v. Wade* abolished any state laws restricting access to abortion. But this legalism can also be seen in the pop culture of the bumper sticker and the radio waves.

One bumper sticker on an evangelical's car read, "God said it. I believe it, and that's that." Another time, going through the dial on the car radio, I picked up an evangelical station. I was struck by the legalistic positivism found in the refrain of one of the songs: "We don't need no philosophies. We got God and His holy decrees." So whether one looks to the high culture of theologians or the low pop culture of the car radio, one encounters the same philosophical approach in the United States, legal positivism buttressed by utilitarianism.

Sadly, in a society shaped by legal positivism and the utilitarian reasoning used to formulate the law, the ones most threatened are the weak and the vulnerable. Sometimes the courts are brutally honest about the implications of the reigning cultural presuppositions of legal positivism. The courts come to determine what is good, what is moral, indeed, what is true. When the Ninth Appellate Court found in *Compassion in Dying v. the State of Washington* that there was a supposed constitutional right for a citizen to engage a physician to help him kill himself, the appellate court referred to the entrenched practice of abortion, established by judicial fiat. The logic is inexorable: if a citizen is free to kill an unborn child who does not ask to die, then surely one is free to kill those who expressly ask for it.

The pervasive reigning cultural attitudes, which give rise to such decisions, determine even the way in which Catholic teaching itself is received. In 1987 the Congregation for the Doctrine of the Faith issued an instruction entitled *Donum Vitae*, "Gift of Life," that provided a moral analysis of different kinds of interventions to overcome infertility. It spoke of the dignity of the human person, of human values and goods. It spoke of the dignity of conjugal intercourse. It was a reasoned reflection on tough questions requiring moral choice. And it said to those interested in the subject, "Come let us reason together. Let us explain why we have had to conclude that some means of overcoming infertility are simply beneath human dignity."

Donum Vitae was not a juridical document. It provided no ecclesial sanctions for individuals who might make use of the means the Congregation judged to be immoral. But before Catholics could even get their hands on the instruction, the elite media in this country supposedly let Catholics know what this was all about. The day the Holy See lifted the embargo on the document, there were all kinds of human interest stories about why the church was repressive and cruel and insensitive by not allowing in vitro fertilization, or surrogate mothering, and so on and so forth. The very day the document was promulgated, the front page of the *Washington Post* declared, "Vatican Bars Many Birth Technologies."[24]

Of course it was not an edict! *Donum Vitae* was not a legal, juridical document. And Catholics could not have rejected it because nobody had had a chance to read it. The television show *Good Morning, America* featured stories on the document the day it was released. It listed the various technologies with a bright red banner across the side of the screen that said simply, "Banned!" Such was not the language or tone of the document of course. *Donum Vitae* pointed out the various affronts to human dignity that could occur within many of these procedures. But once again, the dominant culture was not able even to hear what the Church was trying to say because of its unquestioned coordinates. If the document was being issued by the Catholic Church it must be the arbitrary imposition of the will of those in authority. The only way it could be issued by a religious body is as an arbitrary decree, reflective of the will of the lawgiver.

One of the great challenges we face in responding to the call of the Church for the evangelization of culture is the extent to which the Catholic message will be received in concepts that are not Catholic. That is, in the current cultural context we have to consider the extent to which the Faith will be misunderstood even as it is being preached. Culturally, we tend to attribute to religion the characteristics of a particular religion, that is, Protestantism, which can be characterized as subjective, at times irrational and legalistic.

A number of years ago there was a striking essay in *Time* magazine written by Roger Rosenblatt.[25] He was reflecting on the murder of a head of state, Indira Gandhi, by one of her Sikh guards and the

24. Marjorie Hyer, "Vatican Bars Many Birth Technologies," *Washington Post*, March 11, 1987, A1.

25. Roger Rosenblatt, "Defenders of the Faith," *Time*, November 12, 1984, 112.

murder of a Catholic priest, Jerzy Popieluszko, by Polish Communist agents. What was striking about this essay was Rosenblatt's understanding of religion and how it shaped society. Rosenblatt has a mind that has itself been shaped by our Protestant/secular culture; yet he claims to be writing objectively of religion itself.

"Both killings," Rosenblatt wrote, "involved clashes between the faithful and the state. Faith is belief without reason. Fundamentally religions oppose rational processes." Then he quoted Martin Luther: "Reason is the greatest enemy that faith has. It never comes to the aid of spiritual things but struggles against the divine word, treating with contempt all that emanates from God." Rosenblatt again: "Governments are built and run on exactly opposite bases." One of the points he makes is that there always has to be an opposition between religion and the state. The Catholic idea of building up a human community, of giving recognition to the temporal and the spiritual realism and of them complementing one other and working together for the common good, has no role here. Any colonial city built in New Spain vividly gives expression to the Catholic understanding of the place of religion and government in society. There one has the church and the municipal building right on the same central village square.

In opposition to such an understanding Rosenblatt writes, "Governments are built and run on exactly opposite bases. Governments depend wholly on rational processes. When religions and governments clash, therefore, it is a collision not simply of institutions, but of entirely different ways of apprehending experience." Then he goes on, "All this connects with the American debate on church versus state in a fundamental way. People like Franklin, Washington, Jefferson, and Madison sought to separate church and state so that no one sectarian god would ever bestride the land, yet the founders wanted god somewhere in the picture as a guide to national moral conduct. What the founders did not want, however, was a country run on the basis of religion. America was born of the age of reason. Keeping church and state apart was a way of separating reason and passion, or reason and faith, another check and balance."

Rosenblatt goes on, "Church and state are not merely opposed but actively antagonistic. Faith implies the refusal to accept any laws but God's. How can a government that relies on the perpetuation of its authority be compatible with an institution that takes its dictates from invisible powers?"

This is of course antithetical to Catholic political philosophy. Yet our Catholic faithful are exposed on a regular basis to this kind of thinking. How many of our Catholic faithful would have read that essay in *Time* magazine and had their understanding of the relation between church and state shaped by it? They are taught wherever they turn that it is indeed the nature of religion to be irrational and emotional and superstitious. And of course such an institution ought to be kept out of the public square. It is simply too dangerous. What Rosenblatt did in his essay was to define all religion in terms of Luther's religion. This way of thinking is pervasive in our society. Culturally, our understanding of religion is that of Protestantism.

One encounters the same mind-set recently in the area of the natural sciences. There is a biotech company in Worchester, Massachusetts, that has been attempting to clone human beings. A clone of course is an organism that is a genetic replica of the person who provides the DNA from the nucleus of one of his somatic cells. However, an enucleated ovum is needed for the process. The DNA is removed from the body cell and fused to the enucleated egg. Cell division begins to take place, and the clone begins to grow.

Advanced Cell Technology, the company in question, was taking cows' eggs, enucleating them, and placing the DNA from their scientists' somatic cells into the enucleated ova. The result was Petri dishes with human embryos with cow mitochondrial genetic material mixed in with them.

A personal anecdote may prove illustrative. With some effort I was able to arrange a meeting with the CEO of the company. We had a long and intensive conversation. He was a very earnest, indeed brilliant, individual, committed to doing good. The conversation stretched on for hours. We asked one another how we came to our respective lines of work. He told me that he had grown up as a Nazarene, a very fundamentalist Protestant group. However, he said that he had read every science book he could get his hands on. Then, he said, "I finally reached the point in my life where I came to a crossroads, and I realized I had to choose between God or science." Pointing his finger, he looked at me intently and said, "And I chose God."

He said, "I remember to this day taking my arm and sweeping my science books off the table and onto the floor." Rather stunned, I responded, "But the problem is that you were raised the wrong kind of Christian. No Catholic would dream of having to choose between God and science. All truth comes from one source; revealed truth and scientific truth. There's no opposition between the two."

When I asked what he did next, he said he went off to Harvard to study paleontology. I expressed my surprise since he said he was giving up the study of science. "Well," he said, "I wanted to study paleontology so I could prove the theory of evolution wrong and the book of Genesis right."

Of course he could not do that under those circumstances, and he admitted he couldn't. And so, he said, "I reached the crossroads again between science and religion, and this time I chose science." Indeed, religion was repudiated. But this was an impassioned man, and science became his religion. I said to him again, "I'm sorry. Wrong question, wrong answer. There is no opposition between the two."

I began telling him of the Catholic conviction that there is no opposition between science and religion. He seemed rather startled at this, because I was, after all, the representative of a religion that was supposed to be at odds with reason. I pointed out to him that the pope had recently issued an encyclical entitled *Fides et Ratio,* "Faith and Reason." I indicated that the entire encyclical was on the compatibility between faith and reason, between science and religion. This prominent scientist was astonished that not only would anyone have written a treatise on the compatibility between science and religion, between and faith and reason, but that it would have been done by the pope.

I then told him of *Donum Vitae,* issued by the Holy See in 1987, which provided a moral analysis of the means then available for overcoming infertility. One of the means for overcoming infertility judged to be immoral was cloning. He pointed out that in 1987 most scientists thought it would be impossible to clone a mammal. Dolly the sheep was not cloned until 1997. He was astonished that a Church document appeared to be ten years ahead of the times when it came to a scientific question.

I pointed out that there was an entire section in the Instruction on the moral status of the embryo. This, too, was a matter of great surprise for him. He brought in a group of his scientists to join in the conversation. One was very blunt. "Why would you even waste your time coming out here if you're representing a Catholic organization? What does religion have to do with science?" Admittedly, the prejudices become rather tiring. I stressed again that the Catholic Church sees no incompatibility between the two. "In fact," I said, "the *Catechism of the Catholic Church,* which is the compendium of all the basic beliefs of the Church, defines sin, first of all, not as an act against God's will or God's commandments or God's law. The *Catechism* says, first, sin is an act against reason."[26]

The scientists gathered in that room were incredulous at what I was saying. One asked me to repeat the quote about sin being an act against reason as he wrote it down on his note pad. The cultural problem again was that these people had had their minds shaped by the wrong coordinates. Consequently the Catholic message could barely even be heard.

What is to be done? Nothing short of the total transformation of society according to the mind of Christ, of course! The faith can be maintained only with the greatest difficulty when it is not found within a nurturing culture. That is why from the beginning of his pontificate, John Paul II called for the evangelization of culture. However,

26. *Catechism of the Catholic Church,* n. 1849.

the Faith can be maintained and it can work its effects toward a transformation of society even in the most adverse circumstances.

I had the privilege of providing television commentary on John
Paul's second pastoral visit to the United States. It was like being on
a retreat with him, because I watched his every public action, heard
his every word. And we had advance copies of all of his messages so I
didn't even miss things because of his Polish accent. The visit was one
of the most moving experiences of my life. And I'm convinced at this
point that the only way we can achieve the goals that are so essential
for the perfection of humanity is by looking to the example of this pope
who tried to pattern his life so thoroughly after that of Jesus Christ.

We have to struggle to be as he was, guileless and loving in our
dealings with those around us. We must be willing to be weak and vulnerable and not to fear such a posture, because in our weakness can be
found God's strength. When John Paul addressed the seminarians at
St. Joseph's Seminary of the Archdiocese of New York during his 1995
visit to the United States, he showed how personally and intimately
he could relate with every person there. It was a phenomenal "perfor-
mance" on the part of the pope. He thought he was going to have an
intimate gathering with seminarians. However, when people learned of
the visit, thousands converged upon the seminary. They brought him
in by helicopter, and the crowds immediately pressed in to see him.

However, when he was in the chapel of the seminary, he shut out
all the others, and he addressed just the seminarians. He spoke to them
intimately and directly as men who would one day share in Christ's
priesthood with him, knowing that they would be the ones carrying
the priesthood into the new millennium. "If you do this faithfully," he
said, "teaching the wisdom that comes from above, you will often be
ignored, as Christ was ignored. And even rejected as Christ was rejected. I preach Christ and Christ crucified, says Saint Paul."[27]

And then he got very intimate, "Why has the pope come to Dun-

27. John Paul II, Address at Vespers, St. Joseph's Seminary, New York (October 6,
1995).

nwoody to give you such a serious message? Because, in Christ, you and I, we are friends, and friends can talk about serious matters. If there is one challenge facing the Church and her priests today, it is the challenge of transmitting the Christian message whole and entire, without letting it be emptied of its substance."[28] He asked them to teach the Catholic message in its entirety. Don't be afraid of teaching any of the Christian message, he insisted.

And there was another moment when the pope won the hearts of millions and thereby advanced the evangelization of culture, by diminishing the fear that some have of Christ and his Church. It was another very intimate moment when he was in Central Park with 130,000 people. Only Pope John Paul could turn a gathering with 130,000 into an intimate moment. He was speaking to them as in a conversation, and he reflected on the mystery of Christmas; this was in October. As he was sitting there, he recalled a Christmas carol he would sing in Poland as a child. And he said, "In fact, the pope still sings it." And then this giant of a man, this philosopher, poet, statesman who had helped change the course of human history, this venerable old man, supreme pontiff of the Catholic Church, Vicar of Christ, Bishop of Rome, became as a little child, just like our Lord said was necessary. Before 130,000 gathered in Central Park and millions watching from around the world, the pope became as a child.

Guilelessly and unselfconsciously, he began singing a Christmas carol from his youth. And the result was that all the throng gathered in Central Park themselves became childlike. As he finished his homily, the tens of thousands in Central Park spontaneously began singing a Christmas carol from their own childhood. Everybody together began to sing "Silent Night," unscripted, spontaneous. I believe the Vicar of Christ showed us in that moment that we must become as Christ: nonthreatening, guileless, transparent, honest in our dealings with others, so that they no longer fear Christ and his Church.

Such an attitude on our part will make use of a profound insight

28. Ibid.

that John Paul had into human nature. He was convinced that one of the most profound reasons why people will not come to Christ, and will not lead the moral life, will not allow themselves and their culture to be transformed, is fear. The night of his election to the papacy, he told us, above all else, "Do not be afraid." Throughout his papacy, he told us the same thing. It was a recurring theme during that pastoral visit. And he felt a great urgency in this message.

After the Mass in Central Park he was speaking spontaneously to the people, well before 9/11, and he said "Do not be afraid, be brave." He was speaking spontaneously. "Have courage," he said. "Do not\be afraid."[29] And I was thinking to myself, why is he saying this? What do Americans have to fear? We're the strongest, the most powerful, the most wealthy nation on earth. There is no need to fear starvation or lack of health care or clothing or shelter. What is it that we have to fear? But what indeed?

In our country, defenseless unborn children are so feared that they are destroyed. The young woman is so afraid of loneliness that she climbs into bed with her seducer. The comatose patient is so feared that we want to be able to pull out the feeding tubes. The inconveniences and hardships of marriage are so feared that increasingly spouses and children are left behind through divorce.

If we address our own fears and the fears of this nation with the tenderness, the love, the compassion of Jesus Christ, we will share in his redemption of culture. We will become with him redeemers of culture. The clear, brilliant lights of the Son of Righteousness will then illumine our society so that the truth will no longer be refracted through the cracked lenses of an alien culture. And Mary, the Stella Maris, the Star of the Sea, will replace the wrong coordinates, which have kept us off course, and she will become the sure guide to bring us to the true end of our journey.

29. John Paul II, Homily at Central Park (October 7, 1995).

CONTRIBUTORS

Jude P. Dougherty is dean emeritus and professor emeritus at the School of Philosophy of the Catholic University of America. He holds his degrees from Catholic University, whose faculty he joined in 1967. He has written extensively in metaphysics, social and political philosophy, the philosophy of law, and the philosophy of science. He is editor of the journal *Review of Metaphysics*. Since 1974, he has edited the book series Studies in Philosophy and the History of Philosophy (the Catholic University of America Press), which has published forty-five volumes to date. He has recently authored *Western Creed, Western Identity: Essays in Legal and Social Philosophy* (2000), *The Logic of Religion* (2003), and *Jacques Maritain: An Intellectual Profile* (2003), all published by the Catholic University of America Press.

Kevin L. Flannery was born in Cleveland, Ohio, and entered the Society of Jesus in 1977; he was ordained a priest in 1987. He holds two degrees in philosophy from the University of Oxford: an M.A. and a D.Phil. In 1992, Fr. Flannery began teaching at the Pontifical Gregorian University in Rome, serving as dean of the faculty of philosophy from 1999 to 2005. In 2002, John Paul II appointed him a consulter of the Congregation for the Doctrine of the Faith; in 2005, he was made a member of the Pontifical Academy of St. Thomas Aquinas. His publications include *Ways into the Logic of Alexander of Aphrodisias* (Brill, 1995) and *Acts amid Precepts: The Aristotelian Logical Structure of Thomas Aquinas's Moral Theory* (The Catholic University of America Press, 2001), plus articles on ancient philosophy, on Thomas Aquinas, and on various ethical themes, usually from an Aristotelian or Thomistic perspective.

John Haas is the president of the National Catholic Bioethics Center in Philadelphia, Pennsylvania. He received his Ph.D. in moral theology from the Catholic University of America and his S.T.L. in moral theology from the University of Fribourg, Switzerland. He has served as the John Cardinal Krol Professor of Moral Theology at the St. Charles Borromeo Seminar, Philadelphia, and adjunct professor at the Pontifical John Paul II Institute for Studies in Marriage and the Family, Washington, D.C. In addition to his numerous publications, he is the editor of and a contributor to *Crisis of Conscience* (Herder/Crossroads) and is a contributing editor to *Crisis,* the *St. Austin Review,* and *Touchstone* magazines.

Peter Kreeft is professor of philosophy at Boston College, a noted Catholic apologist, and a prolific author. A former Calvinist Protestant, he entered the Catholic Church in 1959. He holds M.A. (1961) and Ph.D. (1965) degrees from Fordham University, and has taught at Boston College since 1965. He has published more than forty books on philosophy, apologetics, theology, and the writings of C. S. Lewis, Scripture, and spirituality. Some of his recent titles include: *How to Win the Culture War* (Inter Varsity, 2002), *Socrates Meets Jesus* (Ignatius, 2002), *Three Approaches to Abortion* (Ignatius, 2002), *Socratic Logic* (St. Augustine's Press, 2005), and *The Sea Within: Waves and the Meaning of All Things* (Ignatius, 2006).

Richard John Neuhaus is an authority on the role of religion in the contemporary world and is president of the Institute on Religion and Public Life. He has been a leader in organizations dealing with civil rights, international justice, and ecumenism. Fr. Neuhaus is recipient of the John Paul II Award for Religious Freedom. He is editor in chief of *First Things: A Monthly Journal of Religion and Public Life.* Among his best known books are *Freedom for Ministry* (1979), *The Naked Public Square: Religion and Democracy in America* (1984), *The Catholic Moment: The Paradox of the Church in the Postmodern World* (1987), *As I Lay Dying: Meditations upon Returning* (2002), and *Catholic Matters: Confusion, Controversy, and the Splendor of Truth* (2006).

Edmund D. Pellegrino, M.D., is professor emeritus of medicine and medical ethics, a senior research scholar at the Kennedy Institute of Ethics, and adjunct professor of philosophy at Georgetown University, where he was also founder of the Center for Clinical Bioethics. He is chairman of the President's Council on Bioethics and member of the International Bioethics Committee of UNESCO. During his long career, Dr. Pellegrino has served as department chairman, dean, and university president. He is a Master of the American College of Physicians and a member of the Institute of Medicine of the National Academy of Sciences. He has authored over 550 published works, including twenty-four books in medical science, philosophy, and ethics, and is the founding editor of the *Journal of Medicine and Philosophy*.

Robert Sokolowski was ordained a Catholic priest in 1961 and obtained his Ph.D. at the University of Louvain in 1963. Since then Monsignor Sokolowski has taught at the Catholic University of America, where he is Elizabeth Breckenridge Caldwell Professor of Philosophy. He specializes in phenomenology, Greek philosophy, ethics, philosophy of language, and philosophical theology. He has written eight books and over seventy articles, most recently *Introduction to Phenomenology* (Cambridge University Press, 2000) and *Christian Faith and Human Person* (The Catholic University of America Press, 2006). His work has been the subject of conferences at the Catholic University of America (November 1994) and St. Meinrad's Abbey and College in Indiana (April 2000).

Craig Steven Titus is research professor at the Institute for the Psychological Sciences, and research and teaching fellow in the Department of Moral Theology and Ethics, University of Fribourg, in Switzerland. He has written *Resilience and the Virtue of Fortitude: Aquinas in Dialogue with the Psychological Sciences* (2006), edited *The Person and the Polis: Faith and Values within the Secular State* (2006), and coedited *The Pinckaers Reader: Renewing Thomistic Moral Theology* (2005).

INDEX OF SUBJECTS

INDEX OF NAMES

The John Henry Cardinal Newman Lectures
EDITED BY CRAIG STEVEN TITUS

1. *The Person and the Polis: Faith and Values within the Secular State* (2007)

Monograph Series

Fergus Kerr, *"Work on Oneself": Wittgenstein's Philosophical Psychology* (2008)

On Wings of Faith and Reason: The Christian Difference in Culture and Science was designed and typeset in Minion by Kachergis Book Design of Pittsboro, North Carolina. It was printed on 60-pound Natural Offset and bound by McNaughton & Gunn of Saline, Michigan.